A GUIDE FOR BIBLE READERS

Edited by Harris Franklin Rall

THE BOOKS OF THE LAW

A GUIDE FOR BIBLE READERS

Edited by Harris Franklin Rall

THE OLD TESTAMENT

I. The Books of the Law   *Walter G. Williams*

II. The Books of History   *John H. Hicks*

III. The Prophets   *William G. Chanter*

IV. Poetry and Wisdom   *Elmer A. Leslie*

THE NEW TESTAMENT

I. The Synoptic Gospels   *Montgomery J. Shroyer*

II. The Letters of Paul   *Albert E. Barnett*

III. The Acts and Apocalyptic Literature
Edward P. Blair

IV. The Fourth Gospel and the Later Epistles
John Knox

THE BOOKS OF THE LAW

WALTER G. WILLIAMS

ABINGDON - COKESBURY PRESS
New York • *Nashville*

THE BOOKS OF THE LAW
COPYRIGHT, MCMXLV
BY WHITMORE & STONE

Scripture quotations not otherwise noted are from
the American Standard Version of the Revised Bible,
copyright, 1929, by The International Council of Religious Education, and are used by permission.

SET UP, PRINTED, AND BOUND BY THE
PARTHENON PRESS, AT NASHVILLE,
TENNESSEE, UNITED STATES OF AMERICA

TO

My Wife

MARY BUCHANAN WILLIAMS

in appreciation

EDITOR'S PREFACE

THIS volume is intended to help the reader who wishes to know the Bible at first hand. The way to know a country is to visit it and travel through it, not just to read about it. But a good guide can help. He can lead to places of greatest interest and can give information needed for understanding what is seen. The Bible is a great and wonderful country. It is not one book but many books—books in which many voices join, and whose story stretches through many centuries. Its writings differ widely in character, as do the mountains and valleys, the rivers and seacoasts, the cities and plains, of a wide country like ours. At the same time, they have a real unity. They have one source, the Spirit of God moving upon the hearts of men. They have a living center, Jesus of Nazareth. We call the Bible the Word of God, and with good reason, for it comes out of the word which God spoke to these writers "by divers portions and in divers manners," and through it God speaks to us today.

All of us know some parts of the Bible quite well—a chapter here, a verse there, certain psalms learned perhaps in childhood, and some parts of the New Testament. But we all need wider acquaintance with the Bible, and truer understanding and larger appreciation of its wealth of moral and spiritual meaning.

This book is one of eight Guides planned for the purpose of leading to this broader knowledge. The authors have been chosen because of their training in Bible study and their experience in teaching. Four of the books are given to the Old Testament, four to the New. Many of the less important parts of the Bible have of necessity been omitted. The Guides go with the reader on his journey through these writings. They stimulate interest and understanding. They introduce the writer and indicate the time, place, purpose, and special character of the writing. Chapter by chapter, they help the student to discover the meanings and values in the Bible, especially for the personal religious life. Since these Guides will be used largely by ministers, attention is given to material for sermons; but the lay reader will find them equally helpful. Each book is intended to serve for a six months' period. Four or five *Readings* should be completed each week.

Here are some *rules for Bible reading* whose observance will pay rich dividends:

1. Read with a definite purpose and expectation: to understand what is written; to gain quickening of thought and enlargement of mind and vision; to get personal help for good living; and, above all, to meet God and to hear his voice. These are great ends; whether they are reached will rest with each student.

2. Bring all that you have to your reading. What you get will depend on what you bring. Especially, bring a sympathetic imagination. You will not be reading dead words. They came out of life. Try to enter into that life of the past: into the faith of a psalmist and his trials and hopes, the appeal of a prophet speaking to a nation, the witness of Paul, the full heart of the Evangelists. Occasional reading aloud will help make the words live. Bring also an attentive and inquiring mind. Read slowly, pause, reflect, always seeking the real meaning.

3. Read in the spirit of prayer. Offer a prayer as you begin. Ask for the light which God's Spirit can give. Lift up your heart to God and ask God to come to you.

4. Read in the spirit of obedience. Ask what the passage means for your own life and pray for grace to follow what is thus revealed. "Apply thyself wholly to the Bible; apply the Bible wholly to thyself." (Bengel.)

EDITOR'S PREFACE

In this course are frequent references to *ABC*, which means *The Abingdon Bible Commentary*, a commentary on the Old and New Testaments which contains many interesting articles on the Bible as a whole as well as an article on each book of the Bible. The purchase of this book is recommended to the lay reader, who will find it most interesting and helpful. For the minister who is studying these Guides it is indispensable.

The student will find that keeping a notebook from day to day as he reads will prove of great value.

HARRIS FRANKLIN RALL

FOREWORD

AS the following pages were being written I was conscious of the fact that this is not a book in the ordinary sense. These pages are simply the means of sharing religious experiences. As passages of Scripture have been read through the centuries many thoughts have been stimulated, coming from various sources and from many people. It has been my privilege to call these thoughts to your attention in the hope that rich patterns of thought will result in your own mind.

It is not possible to remember always which teachers have suggested this or that, but I wish to take this means of expressing my indebtedness: to Dwight M. Beck, who first introduced me to scholarly research in the Bible; to Leslie E. Fuller, Frederick C. Eiselen, Edwin E. Voigt, and Ernest W. Burch, who deepened my love for Bible study; and to J. M. Powis Smith, William A. Irwin, William C. Graham, and Albert T. Olmstead, under whose leadership I discovered new horizons in the neighboring lands of Bible study.

To Harris Franklin Rall I am deeply indebted. Formerly my teacher, he is now my companion and guide in this endeavor. He has been patient and kind, and from his many years of experience as teacher and writer he has made numerous excellent suggestions and has warned of the pitfalls that await the unwary. I express my appreciation to William K. Anderson and the Commission on Ministerial Training for their selection of Dr. Rall as the editor of this series, as well as for the opportunity afforded me to participate in these studies.

It is a privilege also to acknowledge my appreciation to

11

Mrs. F. Hauser Winter, who has painstakingly and efficiently prepared the manuscript. Her splendid co-operation, in spite of many other demands upon her time, has made possible the completion of this work without undue delay.

To my colleagues I am indebted for many excellent suggestions, and in particular to Professor Martin Rist, who has read most of the typescript.

Finally, I am indebted to my family—Amy, John, George, Eva, and Eddie—who many times have been kept quiet because "Daddy is studying." But more particularly I am grateful for those quick insights and penetrating evaluations of childhood which have contributed so richly to my own understanding of people.

WALTER G. WILLIAMS

The Iliff School of Theology
Denver, Colorado

CONTENTS

INTRODUCTION

THE books we shall study were written by many different individuals, at widely different periods in history, drawing materials from many sources and using many different literary forms and styles. It is possible to give too much attention to the ways in which this body of literature has come together and to overlook the fact that it stands now as one book with a message of God. I shall at times call attention to sources and types of writing, but my major purpose is to help you become acquainted with these books as a part of the Bible, not as fragments of literature.

In the Books of the Law are gathered together the first part of the Bible to be recognized as "Scripture." It is the first division of the Old Hebrew Scriptures. The Jews considered this the most sacred part of their Bible, and still regard it as such. We Protestants have been inclined to put the prophets first. Perhaps we are right in that, but we need to remember that the only way we have of knowing the effect of the prophets' teachings upon the thinking of Israel is to see how Israel applied that teaching in its Law. This we read in the Books of the Law.

This Law is not simply the law of the state, nor religious law, but a combination. It is religion applied to the conditions of man by a people who believed that God was their ruler. There was no separation of church and state in Hebrew times, nor of religion and daily life. The two were intertwined. Late Jewish tradition assumed that all Law had originated with Moses. That is why these Books of Law begin with the story of creation and end with the death of Moses. It is assumed that all Law originated between these two events. Actually, the Law of Israel developed over long

15

periods of time and was not complete until about 400 B.C. It is part of our opportunity to see that development. We shall consider it in some detail in Chapters V and VIII.

For your study Bible use one that will help you most. Choose one having readable type and margins wide enough for notations of significant items and suggestions. Do not be afraid to mark your Bible; it will become more valuable if you do mark it. Some will prefer to use a modern translation such as *The Bible: An American Translation,* published by the University of Chicago Press. In any case, you should have various translations available.

Let the Bible speak to us in everyday language in the hope that religion will be a part of daily living and not something restricted to a special language and special times. We must come to our Bibles for instruction, not for proof of our prejudices. We must let the Bible speak to us instead of asking the Bible to say what we want to hear. Let us read reverently and attentively. Too often, Bible reading becomes a pious but mechanical habit. We feel that "to do our duty" we must read a certain number of verses. We do not read other books this way. Finally, as preachers, we are likely to be always on the search for sermon material. There is a danger here. Our primary purpose in reading the Bible is to undergird our own spiritual lives. When we find inspiration we can bring that inspiration to others. The man who is always looking for strange phrases in order to preach "clever" sermons will fail himself, his people, and his God.

As you read the assignments in your Bible, read also the commentary on these passages in the *Abingdon Bible Commentary,* referred to in this book as *ABC.* At times your attention will be drawn to the more important passages in *ABC,* and special assignments will be made in this commentary.

Three types of questions will be asked in these pages. First, I shall ask questions to stimulate your thinking and to draw attention to significant parts of your reading. In many cases you will want to make notations either in your notebook or in your Bible. Second, I shall raise questions to be answered in your notebook as a part of your study. Finally, there will be the required "Written Work," some of which will be given in the form of questions.

There are nine parts to the Books of the Law:

1. Stories of the beginnings of the world and of men (Gen. 1–11).

2. Patriarchal stories of Abraham, Isaac, Jacob, and Joseph (Gen. 12–50).

3. Moses leading the Israelites from slavery (Ex. 1–18).

4. Laws from Sinai (Ex. 19–40).

5. Laws of the priests (Leviticus).

6. Stories of desert wanderings (Num. 1:1–22:1).

7. In the plains of Moab (Num. 22:2–36:13).

8. Law inspired by prophecy (Deut. 1:1–28:68).

9. The last words of Moses as told by the priests (Deut. 29:1–34:12).

We shall follow this order with a slight rearrangement of titles and groupings; the first *Readings* belong to the first of these divisions. Before beginning *Reading* 1, read in *ABC* pp. 3-10 of "How to Read the Bible" and the article "The Pentateuch—Its Origin and Development," pp. 134-44.

I

IN THE BEGINNING GOD
Genesis 1:1–11:26

OUR Bible begins with the conviction "In the beginning God"—one God. The Christian religion is based upon the fact that there is a God, and only one God. That gives unity of plan and purpose to the universe. It is the basis of all science, and there are many great scientists who say that their work leads them to a belief in God. The Hebrews were the first to discover this great truth. Their neighbors, all the nations around them, believed in many gods. It has been suggested that the Hebrew stories of creation were borrowed from their neighbors. This is probably true. But we are overlooking an important matter unless we see that the Hebrew not only borrowed but changed the story. Originally the story told of many gods. The Hebrew changed this to say "In the beginning God [one God] created." It is a long road over which man has traveled to discover this great truth. In the early days of the Hebrew people they, too, believed in many gods. The work of the great prophets cannot be understood apart from their struggle to enlighten the people in this matter. The Hebrews turned to Baalism constantly, and the prophets fought valiantly to keep their loyalty to Jehovah. Under the influence of the prophetic teachings and the experience of the Babylonian exile the Hebrews came to know that there is only one God.

Today there are eleven great living religions in the world. Only three of these teach a belief in one God. They are Judaism, Christianity, and Mohammedanism. Each of these has its background in the religious literature which a small group of Hebrew people brought back with them from

Babylonian exile. A minority group in possession of a great truth may be God's mightiest means of changing the world.

Reading 1: Genesis 1:1–2:3

There are two stories of creation in Genesis. The story in ch. 1 is the later of the two. It was written by a man who had given much thought to the whole problem of creation. His main purpose was not to give a picture of creation but to explain the origin of the Sabbath. When man first began to observe the Sabbath Day we do not know, but he began very early. The writer of this chapter taught that it was in God's plan from the beginning that there should be a day of rest. Does man need such a day? Can you discover what happens in industry to man's efficiency when he works without a day of rest? Can he rest as well some other day as on the Sabbath? In the modern world, where essential industry must operate seven days each week, can we still observe the seventh day of rest? What are some of the difficulties facing the church in this matter? Notice that this passage says nothing about the Sabbath's being a day of worship. That is a distinctive Christian emphasis.

What kind of world did this writer believe in? Was it round or flat? What does he mean by "the firmament" (v. 7)? Read *ABC*, pp. 126-27 and 219-21. This chapter emphasizes the fact that God in creation brought order out of chaos. Does this tell us anything about God? Was it important to this writer that man was created last?

Read again v. 26. What is meant by the phrase "in our image?" The important word is "image." This writer may have meant a physical image of God. In that case he pictured God as a great giant, manlike in form. It is just as likely that he had in mind our spiritual likeness to God. Which is more important, physical or spirtual likeness? The thought of this likeness might be further developed: God and man as creators; God and man as instruments of love; God and man as instruments of forgiveness; and God and man as moral beings. Note in v. 26 the words "have dominion," which mean "rule." Is this one aspect of our likeness to God? How far has man gone today in his rule over nature? Where has he failed? What about man's control of himself? Here is good sermon material.

Notice also in this chapter that the days are numbered from evening to morning. We count from daybreak to sunset. The Hebrews counted their days from sunset to sunset. That is why the Jewish Sabbath began on Friday evening and continued to Saturday sundown.

All attempts to harmonize this story with the story of creation told by scientists have failed. Does this mean that there is conflict between science and religion? Not at all. It simply means that this writer is not giving us a scientific story of creaton. His great message is religious, and he is necessarily giving us the story in terms of the thinking of his own day, not ours. He says, "God created." Science says that, too. But science gives us a more complete picture and a somewhat different order of events. We cannot think that a man living five centuries before Christ would talk in terms of twentieth century science. If he had done so, the people of his day could not have understood him or his message. God's messengers must always speak in terms which men will understand. There are other creation pictures, or stories, in the O.T.: Psa. 104; Isa. 40; Job 38:4–39:30. Read them; you will find them lofty in thought and noble in language. They are not scientific accounts but great hymns of faith and worship, as are chs. 1 and 2 in Genesis.

Reading 2: Genesis 2:4-14

This second story of creation was written much earlier than that of ch. 1. It is placed second because it is used as an introduction to the story of the temptation of man. Notice how the setting differs from that of ch. 1. The differences are noted in *ABC*, p. 221. Now read *ABC*, pp. 129f., for an explanation of how Bible students identify the various writers.

Attempts have been made to identify the place of the Garden of Eden. All such attempts must fail, for there is no location in all the Near East that would fit the description of the four rivers given in this chapter. The Tigris and the Euphrates can be identified, but there we stop, unless we identify "Gihon" with the Nile. In any case, we know that these rivers do not have a common source.

We are faced with a number of problems. Which of these creation stories shall we follow? In what order did creation occur? Just how was man created? But is it necessary to make a choice between them? If we place our emphasis upon the exact manner of the creation of the world or of man, it would seem so. If we place our emphasis upon the relationship between God and man, then the difficulty of choosing between the stories disappears. The first story of creation emphasizes God as Creator and ends with the hallowing of the Sabbath, on which man may rest. In the second story almost nothing is said about creation. Man is made by his Creator and placed in a garden, but this is simply the preparation for the main part of the story. This we shall study in the next reading.

Reading 3: Genesis 2:15–3:24

One of the problems that has concerned man is "Why do I die?" Many nations in ancient times had stories that gave an answer to that question. This story is the Hebrew answer. Other nations said: "The gods are jealous of man, and they have tricked him out of everlasting life." The Hebrew said: "It is man's own fault." In this story, as in that of the creation, the important matter is not the details of the picture but the truth which it brings. The plain facts are clear. Man has sinned (and sins today). Our great ills come from man's sins, not from God's work and will. The important thing for us is not to quibble about the details of these stories but to get the magnificent insights they give into human nature and the nature of God.

In this story man was created first; woman was created as a companion for man. The animals had been created. In fact, the whole creation came into being for man's delight. Man named the animals, but he found no companion.

Therefore, says this writer, God created woman. The writer seeks to impress upon the reader the close companionship there should be between man and wife. He portrays woman being made from part of man. We should remember that this story is very old, and the version which appears in our Bible was retold in the ninth century B.C. At that time, and for many years afterward, woman was a slave. A man could sell his womenfolk and his children. It was a day, too, when men believed that they could have many wives. A man's wealth was often judged by the number of wives he possessed. Solomon had so many more than other men because he had more money, or drew heavily upon the public treasury. This writer taught that woman was created for a companion and not as a chattel.

The serpent is an object of hatred throughout Hebrew literature. It is portrayed as extremely wise and skillfully deceitful. In the writings of surrounding peoples and in the discoveries of archaeologists, there is much evidence that the reptile was extremely important in the Baal religion, which was a religion of agriculture with emphasis upon magic and fertility. The serpent and his symbol appear frequently. It is quite probable that the extreme hatred of the Hebrew for the reptile arises from this fact. By condemning him constantly through such stories as this, the Hebrew teacher was also condemning one of the chief symbols of Baalism.

Read again carefully the arguments of the tempter. They are well chosen. In our attempts to portray the terribleness of sin we have forgotten that sin is sometimes very attractive and that temptation often comes to us under the most attractive disguises. What were the highly desirable things that the woman wanted? Can you defend her desires? Where was the weakness of the serpent's argument? Can anything be said in favor of the excuses offered by both the man and the woman? Can God forgive sin if there is no confession? What can ministers do when men offer excuses instead of making confession? Write your answers to these questions in your notebook.

Reading 4: Genesis 4:1-24

To understand this story we must have an appreciation for the various types of literature used by the O.T. writers. Read *ABC,* pp. 19-25. Another list of types of writing is given by Professor Robert H. Pfeiffer in his *Introduction to the O.T.* (pp. 24-40) : private and communal songs; narratives; laws, oracles, and prayers; theoretical wisdom, sagas, and legends; folk wisdom, including proverbs, pithy questions, metrical riddles, numerical proverbs, and fables about plants; and literary wisdom, including proverbs of instruction and the books of Wisdom literature. All these forms of speaking and writing were used among the Hebrews just as a preacher today uses such forms as illustrations, quotations of poetry, prose, or a well-known proverb.

This is an old story of the conflict between two ways of life. When the Hebrew people settled in Palestine they changed their ways of living. In the desert they had been wanderers and sometimes shepherds. In Palestine they became settled farmers. Feuds sometimes developed between groups that followed different patterns of life. Cain and Abel represent two types of culture. Abel is pictured as the younger, though actually the wanderer and sheepherder follows the older method of earning a living. The Hebrews came as wanderers into Palestine. When they arrived they found the Canaanite farmer already there. Later the Hebrews changed to the Canaanite method of agriculture. In telling this story, then, it was quite natural for the Hebrews to picture Cain the farmer as the older. He represented Canaanite (possibly Kenite) agriculture. Abel was the younger and represented the newer people, the incoming Hebrews, and of course they taught that the offering of the shepherd was more acceptable to God. Note that nothing is said about the attitude of either man at the time of sacrifice. Cain's anger came *after* he believed that his sacrifice was not acceptable.

Read *ABC,* pp. 75f. and 224-25. How does Cain know that his offering has not been accepted? How does any man know that?

Reading 5: Genesis 6:1–9:29

There are three stories in these chapters: the origin of giants, the Flood, and the curse of Canaan.

As the Hebrews moved about the country they were greatly impressed by the enormous stones they saw. They had been placed in position in an earlier day. Some of them are still standing, monuments to great ingenuity. We now know that they were connected either with places of worship or with burial grounds. We still do not know who placed them there. The Hebrew explanation was that they had been brought there by giants. They accounted for the giants by telling of the union between gods and women. No evidence has yet come to light, however, that giants ever existed in groups in that part of the world. There may have been occasional big men, such as Saul, but he was the exception.

Among the traditions of that ancient world, one of the best known is that of the great flood. It is found among many different nations, and evidence has been found by the archaeologist that the tradition is based upon facts. There was a great flood in the broad spaces that lie between the Tigris and Euphrates rivers, the part of the world that used to be called Mesopotamia and is now known as Iraq. How widespread the flood was we do not know. The story, as it is told here, is an interweaving of several strands of older stories. In general, we may say that the more primitive parts of the story are by the Judean writer, while the Priestly writer has added many details of construction, definite dates, and measurements. Differences may be noted between v. 6:20, 7:2, and 7:4. Did one pair or seven pairs of each kind go into the ark? How long did the Flood last, forty days or one year?

One of the most interesting parts of the Hebrew story of the Flood is that of the interpretation of the rainbow. Notice that the purpose of the rainbow is to remind God of his promise, not man (vv. 14-15). That is a simple picture of God, but because of this story the rainbow now became

25

for the people a symbol of God's promise. God had a concern for his people.

The third story is a mixture of blessing and curse. It attempts to account for the bitter feeling between the Hebrews and the Canaanites. A full explanation is found in *ABC*, p. 227. It remains only to add that it seems unfair to curse a grandson because of what his father has done. It is possible that when the Hebrews saw the drunken orgies of the Baal religion among the Canaanites they saw in them the curse of the man who first cultivated the vine.

Reading 6: Genesis 10

Ch. 10 is an attempt to draw the surrounding peoples into one picture. All nations are portrayed as descendants of one family of three sons, Shem, Ham, and Japheth. Some of these peoples can be identified, but many of them are still unknown. They undoubtedly existed, or at least were still known by name, at the time of this writing. We could not agree with this classification of nations from what we know of skeleton measurements and language relationships. The only means of classification known at that early time was where people lived, not what language was spoken. (Other scientific methods of classification were unknown.) Our present term "Semite" comes out of this chapter. The name "Shem" was pronounced in some quarters as "Sem," and the supposed descendants of Shem have come to be known as Semites. According to our present knowledge there are a number of inaccuracies in this account. Canaan is called a descendant of Ham, but we know that Canaanites were Semites. Canaan is also named as the father of Heth. The Hethites, better known as Hittites, were not Semites. The Philistines are shown to be descended from Egypt, but this does not agree with history. What then is the purpose of this list? Simply to provide a link between the nations then existing, and to prepare for the story in 11:10-26, showing Abraham to be descended from Noah by way of Shem.

Let us note also that as these nations are listed it is stated that each had its own language (vv. 5, 20, 31). Presumably the event in 11:1-9 was thought to have preceded ch. 10. We need to remember that the ancient storyteller was not concerned with the order in time. It was enough that as he told each story his hearer would call another to mind. Perhaps this is a more interesting way of telling stories. Read *ABC,* pp. 114f.

Reading 7: Genesis 11:1-9

This delightful story is Babylonian in its background. Not only is the city of Babylon mentioned, but the tower and the method of its construction are definitely Babylonian (see *ABC,* p. 228a). It should be added not only that such towers are known through archaeology but also that we know by reading Babylonian clay tablets something of the religious thinking connected with these places. They were man-made mountains, and these people thought that their gods actually lived on top of them. So far as Babylonian thinking was concerned, such a structure was an attempt on man's part not to invade heaven but rather to make a place of residence for God among men. The Hebrew tells this story to explain why men speak different languages. Contrast the difference between the diversity of mankind portrayed here and the unity of mankind for which Christianity is striving today. Yet the Hebrew was not wrong when he emphasized the great difference between God and man.

Written Work.—Write a brief sermon, based on the suggestions in *Reading* 1, on "The Image of God in Man." State what this means and what obligation this lays upon us for our own lives and for our treatment of other men.

II

ABRAHAM, ISAAC, AND JACOB
Genesis 11:27–37:1

AS WE turn to the story of Abraham we are treading for the first time upon historical ground. Many events in connection with the life of Abraham have no basis for historical comparison, but there are others which can be checked. We can establish with reasonable accuracy the time of Abraham, and from clay tablets and other sources we know much about the period in which he lived. Roughly we may place Abraham in the early part of the second millennium, about 1900 B.C. Some historians date him as early as 2100 B.C., and others would bring him down as late as 1750 B.C.; but if we say shortly after the turn of the twentieth century before Christ, we shall not be far astray.

Ch. 12 begins the second part of the story of God's people. After the creation and early preparation for his coming, the main ancestor is introduced to the story of Israel. We shall note that some of the stories associate him with Ur of the Chaldees. Chaldea was the name applied to southern Babylonia, not far from the Persian Gulf. It was used only after the new Babylonian empire had come into being toward the close of the seventh century B.C. The name Chaldea, then, indicates that these stories in their present form were written not earlier than the seventh century. Other stories of Abraham and his family associate them with Haran, nearly four hundred miles northeast of Jerusalem and about two hundred miles west of Nineveh, the capital of the Assyrian empire. The constant movements of Abraham and the family indicate that they were wandering Aramaeans who lived on the fringes of civilization. They seem to have moved around what Professor Breasted has called "The Fertile Crescent." Watch for references to Abraham as a tent dweller. He corresponds closely to the present-day tribal sheik. Read *ABC,* pp. 73-76.

Ezekiel said: "By origin and birth you belong to the land of the Canaanites. Your father was an Amorite, and your mother a Hittite" (16:3—*American Trans.*). In Deuteronomy also we read: "You shall solemnly declare before the Lord your God, 'A nomad Aramean was my father.'" (26:5—*American Trans.*). These and other passages indicate that the early Hebrews recognized their nomadic and desert origin. They confessed that they were a mixed people. Only later did they insist that they were a pure "race" and that it was forbidden them to intermarry with "foreigners." The story of Abraham indicates that the earlier memory of the people was correct.

These records of Abraham are records of tribal groups that later became the Hebrew people. So far as history can check the record of the Hebrew people, then, it begins with a man and his family who left his homeland and settled in a far country. Why did he go? We wish we had more information at this point. The record simply says to "make of thee a great nation" (12:2). We like to believe that since he was convinced that he was God-sent, he therefore journeyed because of religious conviction. (See Heb. 11: 8-10.)

Reading 8: Genesis 11:27–13:18

The Bible tells an honest story of its heroes. Sometimes we look on these men as saints, but they were not. They were very human and had many weaknesses. Our Bible makes no attempt to gloss over the weaknesses of these men. In this respect our Bible differs from other sacred writings. Yet, in spite of the faults of these men, God was able to use them for his purposes. Let us remember, too, that these men must be judged by the standards of their own day, not according to standards of the twentieth century A.D. There are those who insist that the world does not change—or if

29

it does, it is getting worse. Evangelism is possible only as we realize that men's lives can be changed. History affirms that changes have been made in men's thinking and that the moral standards of the world today are far higher than they were forty centuries ago. Make comparisons of the standards of living, the treatment of enemies, the status of women and children, and the concepts of God held then and now. Those changes have come because of religion.

The land of Canaan was Abram's first stop after leaving Haran (12:5). Locate Bethel and Ai on your map. Read *ABC*, pp. 52f. Why did Abram build altars at these places? Did churches exist in that day? What was the form of worship in that day? Did Abram act as the priest for his family? Were services held regularly, or did men worship when they felt the need? Have we become too rigid in our expressions of religion today?

Famine is a frequent visitor to Palestine, and Egypt has long been the bread basket of the East. When famine came to Abram in Palestine, his next stopping place was Egypt. The account of Abram and his wife is given to indicate how much more beautiful Sarah was than Egyptian women. Note that the same story is told with some change of detail in ch. 20 and again in ch. 26, this time about Isaac. In each case the offender made an excellent gain of property through his deceit. Morality was not the chief concern in that day. There is another difficulty. In ch. 12 Sarah is already sixty-five years of age, and in ch. 17 she is more than ninety! Could the Pharaoh have been interested in a woman of that age?

Ch. 13 portrays Abram in a better light. Let us note, however, that Abram does not give land to Lot. It is not yet his. He gives Lot only the choice of direction, and Lot then has to get possession of the land. It is only after Lot leaves that we read of God's giving the land to Abram. Here again we must get the right emphasis. It is on the great number of descendants promised to Abram rather than on the lands he is to have.

Reading 9: Genesis 16:1–17:27

Chs. 16-17 are concerned with two things of importance in the religion of the Hebrews, the origin of the nation and the origin of circumcision. The promise of a son to Abram is important. If Abram is to be the father of a great people he must begin with a son. Sarai, his wife, was barren, a terrible condition for any Semite. Semites believed that such a woman was in disfavor with God. God alone could change the condition. There was a step that society had planned so that families would not become extinct. A wife could give her maid to her husband and any child resulting from that union would be considered the child of the wife, not of the maid. Sarai took this step now. It led to jealousy.

There is another phase of the narrative, to account for characteristics of the Ishmaelites. See *ABC,* pp. 230-31.

Names have great significance in the Near East. They are usually descriptive of the relation of the parents or the child to God. Americans usually name children for some close kin, but the Hebrews did not. Note for instance the explanation of the name of Ishmael. Three names are changed in ch. 17. First, Abram learns a new name for God. The significance of "El Shaddai" (v. 1 mg.) is not clear. It may mean "God Almighty," but it is more likely that it meant "God of the fields." The name is used by Jews today. It is the name that is printed to appear in the window of the emblem given by Jewish chaplains to servicemen. We may be certain that Abram understood through this name that God had certain essential powers. Next, Abram's name is changed to Abraham. Undoubtedly there is a play on words, the significance of which has not yet been discovered. Finally, the name Sarai is changed to Sarah. Again the increased importance of the individual is indicated by a changed name.

The major part of ch. 17 is devoted to a record of the rite of circumcision, and it is entirely a priestly account. In Exodus the account of the circumcision of Moses' son implies that this rite had its origin in the nature religion

31

and that it was very old, flint knives being used. The writer indicates that this rite was understood as one of the signs of covenant relationship. Notice how many times the Hebrew uses acts of daily life to remind himself of his relation to God. That is good religious education. Perhaps this explains the tenacity of Hebrew culture.

Reading 10: Genesis 18:1–19:29

Four accounts are given attention in these two chapters. The first deals with the promise to Abraham of a son. The second is the intercessory prayer of Abraham. The third is a description of the unnatural cravings of the men of Sodom. Finally, there is told the story of the escape of Lot and his family from destruction. A brief story is appended to show that the Moabites and the Ammonites, enemies of Israel, are the result of incest.

The charm of the first story is its simplicity. Its true Oriental character is indicated in *ABC,* p. 232*a.* It is from this story that the expression "to entertain angels unaware" has come. It has been pointed out what an opportunity Abraham would have missed if he had been ungracious to the strangers. Contrast the hospitality of the desert with the indifference of modern city living.

Another great characteristic of Abraham is indicated in the second account. Overcoming his fear of God, Abraham pleads for the lives of the people. They are people he does not know. We have here the ideal of man making intercessory prayer.

The third account begins with the gracious hospitality of Lot. The contrast between the depravity of the men of Sodom and the concern of Lot for his guests is striking. Note, however, the extremely low place that woman had at that time in the scale of values. The purpose of this account is to give the setting for the destruction of Sodom and Gomorrah.

The destruction of those cities was a thing to be remembered down through the generations. Recent investigations

32

by the Standard Oil Company indicate that these cities were destroyed by a combination of earthquake and fire, the fire made more terrible by the seepage of oil and bitumen from the ground. The Hebrew explanation for the destruction was simply that God had sent destruction because of the sinfulnes of the city. It has led many people to say that any natural catastrophe is sent by God to punish men for their sins. Dare we make such a statement after hearing the teaching of Jesus that God is love?

Reading 11: Genesis 21:1–22:19

This familiar account has been retold many times, and yet it is possible that we have overlooked one of the most significant phases of the record. This story comes from a time when there was frequent human sacrifice. Early records indicate that it was the practice to offer not only the first fruits of the ground, but all first-born males, animals and human. A number of passages indicate the prevalence of the practice in various forms: 2 Kings 3:27; Mic. 6:7; Lev. 27:28; Judg. 11:31, 34. It may be that in this account of Abraham is recorded man's first conviction that God does not desire human sacrifice. We cannot overlook the fact that Abraham was willing to sacrifice that which was nearest and dearest to him. Let us, however, raise the question, Was this not also an offering of Sarah's? To be sure, according to the customs of the day she would have no voice in the matter. Nevertheless, her heart would ache as much as Abraham's. This is another indication of the low status of woman at that period.

Written Work.—Prepare one of these two assignments: (1) Write a description of Abraham, giving the good and the bad sides of his character. Write a similar description of Lot. Is he any better or any worse than Abraham? Give the reasons for your answer. Can we say Abraham was a religious pioneer? (2) Write a sermon outline on "Religious Pioneers." Read Heb. 11:8-10.

Reading 12: Genesis 24:1-61

As Abraham approached the close of his life he was concerned that his son Isaac should marry. How could there be a great nation without his son's marriage? He called his trusted servant and commissioned him to find a wife among the kinsfolk back in Haran. The servant made an oath in the manner that was most binding—by placing his hand under Abraham's thigh. Oriental custom is reflected in this account, for it was the father's prerogative to find a wife for his son. The son had no choice. Similarly, the girl had no voice, usually, in the matter. Undoubtedly, there were other high-spirited girls besides Rebekah who had ways of indicating whether or not they were satisfied with the agreements. Another indication of the human interest in this story is the manner of choice. Was she a good water drawer? One of the main functions of the housewife in the East is to provide the household with water. Being a good procurer of water was a real asset. Even in these days, Arabs select their brides according to their ability to carry water. The servant made selection first upon her ability as a housekeeper, then upon her appearance. Only after he was satisfied at these points did he inquire about her family. Laban, on the other hand, was more interested in the quality of the gifts that Rebekah had received. On that basis alone he welcomed the visitor (see *ABC,* pp. 77f.). Now notice the close relationship of Rebekah to Isaac. Her father was a cousin of Isaac. But Abraham had married his half-sister, so there would be no barrier at this point.

Notice the common courtesies extended to the visitor. The important thing was to make the guest comfortable. Notice how many of these stories mention the washing of feet. After a traveler crossed dusty roads, and perhaps desert, with sandal-shod feet, washing of the feet was necessary; and nothing rested the visitor more than such an act.

The wedding plans were made. It remained only for the servant to settle the matter of dowries, and this is undoubtedly reflected in the account of the presents given to the prospective bride and her parents. Now she is ready to follow the servant to her husband.

Reading 13: Genesis 25:19-34; 27:1-41

We begin now the story of Jacob. The Aramean background of the family is again recognized in the formula of v. 20. Immediately we are thrown into the controversy between Jacob and Esau. Esau was the first-born, yet we always refer to "Jacob and Esau." Note again the significance of names among the Semites. Esau's name meant possibly "the hairy one"; and later it is indicated that his name was changed to "Edom," meaning "red." This is preparation for the later accounts of conflict between Israel and Edom. The familiar "mess of pottage" story carries out the same idea of conflict. The right to inheritance and the paternal blessing belonged to the first-born. Here the principle is applied to the nations, with the indication that Edom, descended from the first-born Esau, forfeited its rights to Israel, descended from Jacob.

Ch. 27 continues the contest between Jacob and Esau. We should say that the deceit of Jacob was immoral. The emphasis in this story, however, is not on morals, but on the cleverness of Jacob. Jacob may have said to himself: "The blessing belongs to me. I bought it from Esau. It is a part of the birthright, and I am justified in taking any measure to get it." To understand the significance of the "blessing," we must remember that only one such blessing could be given by the father and that it normally belonged to the first-born. Notice that the blessing (27:39b-40) is in verse. It is very old and has existed long enough to be shaped into fine verse. It has become one of the firm traditions of the tribes.

Note, too, that the blessing is one that a farmer would give to his son. It is not a wanderer's blessing, nor the blessing of the hunter. Let us remember, too, that there are interwoven here the traditions of a family and the traditions of the early tribes. This record was written down at a time when the Hebrews were settled on the land and Edom was a wandering restless people.

It may be that when these poems were sung around the campfires the hearers thought not of Isaac and his family but of the nation in the south, an enemy group. This is an early form of nationalism, and among nations cleverness still seems to be more desirable than morals.

Reading 14: Genesis 29:31–30:24

Historians agree that the Hebrew people had their origin in a confederation of tribes that later became a nation. One of the earliest confederations is that recorded in the Song of Deborah, but the tribes listed in the song do not agree with the traditional list of the tribes.

Very early the twelve-tribal pattern became basic thinking in Hebrew history. A careful reading of these chapters will give a clearer understanding of the later attitudes toward certain tribes, particularly concubine tribes, that is, the tribes descended from the servants of Leah and Rachel.

Two changes occurred in the list of the tribes at an early period. First, the Levi tribe was dropped with the explanation that they were set aside for sacred service. Then, to restore the number to twelve, Joseph's sons, Ephraim and Manasseh, are substituted for the Joseph tribe. These tribes are referred to as half-tribes. Note the significance of the names of the tribes. This is in agreement with Semitic tradition. In the tablets found at Ras Shamra, a village on the north Syrian coast, were some listing names of contributors to the temple. These lists were from the fourteenth century B.C. Among the names are some which may be translated "When the well fell in," "The night of the storm," and so on. Such names are strange to us but were perfectly normal in that ancient day. Notice again the struggle for motherhood. The servant's children were considered the children of her mistress. For the twelfth son, or tribe, it is necessary to go over to Gen. 35:18.

This writer is an excellent storyteller. Note how he maintains the suspense. His hearers knew that Joseph and Benjamin had to get into that account somehow, but he saves their names till last.

Reading 15: Genesis 30:25–31:54

In the contest of wits between Jacob and Laban, Jacob is easily the victor. Much may be said in justification of Jacob's acts, since it is clear that Laban continually sought to take advantage of him. And we must be careful to view this story, as others, in the light of the moral standards of that day, not our own. Nevertheless, we find it difficult to exonerate Jacob of all blame.

There are three parts to this record. First, there is the attempt of Laban to keep Jacob in his service. Apparently Jacob was a good workman and Laban was anxious not to lose him. Jacob took advantage of the situation, and made sure that in the breeding of animals the advantage came to him. His own flocks were built up, but Laban's did not fare as well. After building his fortune, for flocks were a man's wealth in that day, he decided to leave for Palestine. Second, there is Jacob's flight. At a time when Laban was away at a distance of three days' journey Jacob and his family started on their long trek to their new home. Meantime, Rachel stole the family gods. It has been pointed out that this is another indication that in this period they believed in many gods. We need to notice also that the possession of the household gods was extremely important. In 31:15 we see that Jacob and Rachel knew they had been cut from any inheritance to which they may have been entitled. "Now," they say, "we are considered as foreigners." Clay tablets from this period indicate that the possession of the family gods carried also the right of inheritance, so Rachel was taking the idols not because of any particular religious sentiment but solely to protect her rights of inheritance. Because of Rachel's cleverness the search by Laban when he finally caught them was unsuccessful. The third phase is the partial reconciliation of Laban and Jacob. The atmosphere was cleared as each man presented his side of the argument. Finally there was agreement, and a covenant. At the risk of spoiling what has come to be a beautiful benediction, we must in fairness note that the original meaning of the covenant was "The Lord keep his eye on us when we are out of each other's sight." Old words take on new significance as new religious experiences are allowed to add to their meaning. Meditate upon the tremendous strides that have been taken by man along the road of religion from that day to this. Our thought as we use this blessing now is that we commit each other in love to the watchful care of God. Could such a change as that have been possible unless men had discovered the love of God through Jesus? What other changes have come about since Jacob's day?

Reading 16: Genesis 31:55–32:32

Chapter and verse division in the Bible is usually quite helpful, but occasionally the divisions come at the wrong place. Here the closing verse of ch. 31 belongs quite naturally with the record in the next chapter. Our earliest MSS. of the Bible indicate that there were no such divisions in the original writings of the Bible. These were added much later simply for ease of reference. Modern printings of the Bible put these chapter and verse divisions into the margin, for they are actually marginal references, not a part of the original plan of writing. Let us use them for aids in finding our way around in this library of books. They must not be "stop" signs in reading.

Two matters of great importance demand our attention in this reading. First, there is the serious preparation by Jacob for a meeting with his brother Esau. Word came to him that Esau was on the march with four hundred men. To Jacob that meant trouble. Perhaps his conscience bothered him. His means of appeasement was to make such a generous gift to his brother that he would disarm him, and Esau would not steal the remainder of the flocks of Jacob. The outcome is left to a later chapter.

Then comes the story of Penuel (32:24). This is a story that was told and retold to explain why the Hebrews did not eat a certain part of the hip meat. The interest for us is not in the explanation of this Jewish dietary law but in Jacob's experience and his religious concepts. Whether the experience is a dream or not is relatively unimportant. Jacob suddenly became conscious of divine presence. During that time he raised the question, "What God are you? Please tell me your name." Why should he ask that question? Jacob was traveling through a strange land, and he did not know the names of the gods of that land. In that day it was believed that each country had its own gods, and the gods were limited in their power to their own territory. It was important, then, to learn the name of this divine being. Jacob received no answer, but he was told that his own name was to be changed from "Jacob" to "Israel." In 35:10 we have another record of the change in Jacob's name. It may be that both are attempts to bring together the traditions of two groups of people under a common ancestor.

Reading 17: Genesis 34:1-29

This story of the revenge of Dinah's brothers is revolting to modern ears. It is another evidence of the much lower standards of an early day in the history of man. A few things must be noted to understand the significance of this account. It may reflect conflict between tribal groups as suggested in *ABC*, p. 241; but in its present form the story stands in terms of individual relationships and reflects individual moral standards. The concern of the men of the family was largely economically motivated. Women were chattels in that day, and a violation of their person resulted in a lowering of the marketable value. How greatly different is the standard of Christianity, which stresses the sanctity of human personality! The later portions of this story do show man's growing concern for morality.

Next we shall notice that the men of that day felt perfectly satisfied that their trickery should lead to the death of all men of the city. They lived in a day when men believed that it was smart military strategy to accomplish such an act. If the enemy had done it they would have cried aloud that it was treachery. That was nearly four thousand years ago.

Written Work.—Write a brief sermon showing how religion changes men's standards of what they should be and what they should do. Your text might be "Grow . . . in knowledge" (2 Pet. 3:18). Read carefully Mt. 5:38-45. Point out some of the lower standards shown in these O.T. accounts. Note how Jesus corrects and criticizes. What makes the difference? Where do we as Christians get our standard?

III

JOSEPH AND THE EGYPTIANS
Genesis 37:2–50:26

MUCH information is now available to us about the Egyptians in the period of the patriarchs. There were great movements of peoples in the middle of the second millenium B.C. A people referred to in history as the Hyksos moved down the Palestine coast and into Egypt. They took possession of the Egyptian throne. The Kyksos were a conglomeration of many peoples apparently, but as they pushed through Palestine they became predominantly Semitic. The result was that in the period when Joseph, and later his family, went to Egypt there was a ruling caste that was favorable to the Semites. The Joseph stories are a part of the cherished traditions of the later Hebrews. We shall note a number of Egyptian influences in this cycle of stories.

Slavery was a common thing in that day. Many of the Egyptian monuments picture slaves at work. The erection of great buildings and the movement of enormous pieces of stone was possible only because there was an almost inexhaustible supply of slave labor. Many writers have suggested that the Egyptians were greatly advanced in engineering as evidenced by the erection of the great pylons, "Cleopatra's Needle," the pyramids, and other structures. That may be, but it must be borne in mind that such building feats were more the result of huge forces of slave labor than of skillful engineering. The monuments portray many foreign people as slave laborers, including the Semites. Slaves were used, too, in the turquoise mines in Sinai. In this case, we know that the labor was heavily Semitic.

One human tendency has led to confusion in this part of

the history of the Hebrew people. It is the universal desire to share in glories of the past. So many Americans insist that their ancestors came over in the "Mayflower" that it must indeed have been a large boat. Similarly, when the rescue from Egyptian slavery became the great demonstration of God's purpose and power, all tribes insisted that they had shared the experience. A careful check of the Bible records shows that only a few people went to Egypt, and a relatively small group emerged. The experience was probably confined to the Joseph tribes. In all likelihood, for about two hundred years *before* the liberation of the Joseph tribes from Egypt there were Semites pushing in across Jordan and settling in Canaan. They, too, became a part of the later Hebrew confederacy. A recognition of this overlapping will help to clear many problems that have confronted us of the supposed conflict of the Bible record with what the archaeologist has discovered in other records.

Reading 18: Genesis 37:2-36

God sometimes must use unpromising material. As we read the opening description of Joseph, he is far from attractive to us. His own family knew him as a tattler, a conceited and smug half-brother. He was unwanted and perhaps feared. It would be difficult to account for the brothers' plans to kill him unless there were deep hatreds born of fear. Reuben and Judah have the maturity that can come with age, and compared with Joseph they are far greater characters. Yet Joseph had the raw materials necessary for strong leadership. Handicaps would not deter him; they would spur him to his goal. He had the possibility of becoming a tyrant or a trusted leader of men. Was religion the determining factor in his life? We know very little about the religion of Joseph, but we do know something about his character; and character indicates the worth of a man's religion. List the good and the bad characteristics of Joseph and his brothers in this story.

V. 35 contains the first mention of Sheol in the Bible. This was translated "grave" or "hell" in the A.V. (Authorized, or King James, Version), but the Hebrew literally refers to "the place of abode of all departed." The ancient Hebrews believed that when a person died his outworn spirit went down under the earth to a place named "Sheol." Everyone went there at death. It was not a "life after death" but simply a place of deposit for outworn spirits. In this depository there was no distinction between good and bad. Many times we read, "And he was gathered to his fathers." This was another expression for death and indicated the same fact—namely, that all went to the same place. For the ancients, a man's life was rewarded or punished here upon the earth, not in an after life. A good man lived a long life, but the evil man died an early death. In the Commandments, reward is indicated by the phrase "that thy days may be long in the land which the Lord thy God giveth thee" (Ex. 20:12). In the patriarchal period, an old man was thought to be very good and extremely wise. This was one of the fundamentals of patriarchal society. Notice in v. 34 the means of expressing sorrow. Burial and mourning customs are discussed in *ABC,* p. 76.

Reading 19: Genesis 38:1-30

Ch. 38 interrupts the narrative of Joseph. It is a very old story and can be understood only in the light of social, moral, and religious patterns of many centuries ago. In two major respects social customs in that day were greatly different from those of today. The first is the provisions that were made by society to insure the ongoing of the family and tribe. If a man died childless, his widow was given in marriage to a brother. The first child resulting from their union was considered the child of the first husband. By this means, men had children to tend their graves and to perpetuate their memory. Tamar's conduct indicates how imperative she felt was the demand of this law. (See Deut. 25:5-10 and the discussion "On Levirate Marriage," *ABC,* p. 337a.)

The other great change in social and religious customs indicated in this story is the attitude toward extramarital relations. Tamar pretends to be a temple devotee. It was a very common practice in the Baal religion for women to devote their bodies in the name of religion. Payments received by them belonged to the temple of the Baal. There was no censure; it was an accepted practice. Hosea is the first religious leader to denounce this practice for what it really was—harlotry. Note that there is no condemnation of the "woman by the wayside" nor of Judah. Tamar is strongly denounced when it was assumed that she was guilty of harlotry. The penalty was death by stoning. But this condemnation comes to her as a widow in Israel, not as a follower of Baal. Judah was not condemned even when he admitted he was father to her child. Standards were lower, and there was one standard for men and another for women in those days. The very fact that the Hebrew word which means "sacred woman" was later translated "harlot" shows the great strides taken by mankind. The first man to fight for this changed attitude was the prophet Hosea. When evil acts are carried on in the name of religion, or with the approval of religion, they are far more difficult to eradicate. This is why governments, political parties, merchants of questionable products, and others are anxious to receive the approval of the church. Nothing becomes good or bad simply because it receives approval or condemnation of the church, but we must remember that many people assume that this is true. For this reason, every religious leader is under moral obligation to be certain of his facts before he praises or condemns acts of public or private conduct. This also is why it is imperative that no religious group or organization should ever permit in its name any program or procedure of questionable character. We dare not underestimate the importance of religious leadership.

Reading 20: Genesis 39:1-23

Many years are covered quickly in the opening six verses of ch. 39. Joseph grows from boyhood to manhood. His character has developed along with his body. Try to imagine the many different jobs held by Joseph before he became the overseer, or superintendent, of Potiphar's household. What characteristics of Joseph appealed to Potiphar? What sort of man was Potiphar? In the middle of v. 6 there is an interesting sidelight on his nature. The phrase may well be translated thus: "He had no concern for anything except the food he ate."

Another interesting character study may be made of Potiphar's wife. She evidently loves Joseph passionately, for when he makes no response to her advances her love turns to anger and hatred. Joseph's determination does not falter when he finds himself trapped and his reputation and his job torn from him. He does not whine or revolt when he is thrown into prison, but by hard work he wins the esteem of his jailer.

Vv. 5, 9, 21, and 23 give us the secret of Joseph's moral strength. Does Joseph refrain from evil because of fear, because of moral conviction, or because he understands that God will reward good conduct? The record simply says that Joseph was convinced that God was the secret of his success, and refused to sin against God.

Written Work.—Write a paper comparing the characters of Jacob, Joseph, and Potiphar. What was the significance of religion in the life of each?

Reading 21: Genesis 40:1-23

The ability to interpret dreams was considered by the ancients a sign of God's special favor. Even as late as the close of the seventh century B.C. the Hebrew law codes catalogued dreams as one of the means of discovering God's will. The prophets, however, knew that the will of God for man's life was not mysterious but very simple: it was "to do justly, and to love mercy" (Mic. 6:8—A.V.) . The common man could know that will. And to do that will was the important matter, not to try to probe the future by such means as dreams.

Dreams are important. Students of the human mind tell us that frequently the tensions in an individual's life are reflected in his dreams. The psychiatrist may investigate our

45

dreams when other examinations fail to discover what problems are troubling us most. But ancient man knew—as well as moderns—that dreams are man-centered and not God-centered. Men later learned to distrust dreams, portents, and their interpretations. In Joseph's day it was thought that dreams were God-sent, and that they could best be interpreted by men of God's own choosing. The ability of Joseph to interpret the dreams of his jail companions was proof positive that he was a favorite of the Deity.

How human the butler turned out to be! He forgot all about Joseph in his joy at being restored to his old job. What were Joseph's feelings as he realized the thoughtlessness of the butler? How many people can you think of who would be angry in such a circumstance? How many would be contented that they had befriended someone, however ungrateful he proved? Which are in the majority? Are we always careful to remember those who have been of help to us?

A few wise preachers have discovered that to remember a kindness makes church machinery run more smoothly, particularly if the acknowledgement is made in the presence of others. This is not insincerity or "politics." It is simply the recognition that most of us are more responsive to praise than to censure. The most famous short story in all literature, the parable of the good Samaritan, has its climax in the praise of the Samaritan rather than the condemnation of priest or Levite. That is its greatness.

Reading 22: Genesis 41:1-46a

There came a time when the butler did remember what Joseph had done for him. It was to his advantage to inform Pharaoh about Joseph when the magicians and wise men had failed. ("Pharaoh" was really a title, like king or emperor, not a personal name, and it would be more accurate to write "the pharaoh" instead of Pharaoh.) Pharaoh probably rewarded the butler together with Joseph. In any case,

Joseph would not be likely to forget the butler. The main stress of the story is that Joseph in the name of the God of Israel was far wiser than all the wise men and magicians of Egypt. That was a day in which men still believed in many gods, each nation having its own. For Joseph to solve what the others could not was sure evidence, at least to the Israelites, that their God was superior to the gods of Egypt.

Joseph is here credited with discovering through the dream that there is a cycle of prosperous and depression years. One American economist insists that he discovered his principle of the economic cycle by reading this story of Joseph. How early man discovered the wisdom of saving for the lean years we do not know, but we know from Egyptian monuments that Egypt built storehouses at least a thousand years before the time of Joseph. An inscription cut in rock tells us that the reserve supply is gone because for seven years the Nile has not overflowed and herbage has therefore failed. The incident is in the reign of King Zoser of the third dynasty in the thirtieth century B.C., but the date of the inscription is in the second century B.C. Egypt apparently remembered stories of the seven-year cycle.

The Egyptians did not wait to see whether or not the word of Joseph would prove to be true. Joseph was so convincing that he was given the immediate authority necessary to conserve surplus grain for time of need. The only period in which a Semite would have been given great power was during the supremacy of the Hyksos over the Egyptians in the seventeenth and early part of the sixteenth centuries B.C., a circumstance which fits, but does not prove, the Bible account.

Joseph became completely Egyptian. He was given an Egyptian name and he married the daughter of a priest of the Egyptian religion. His religion also was undoubtedly influenced by his Egyptian life and friends. But the Hebrews remembered that Joseph's success was due entirely to the God of Israel.

47

Reading 23: Genesis 41:46b–42:17

To get the greatest enjoyment and inspiration from the story of Joseph, read in a modern translation the complete story from Gen. 41:46 to 46:30 (but omitting 46:8-27). Here is storytelling at its best. What boy will not thrill to this adventure and wait with delight for the climax of the story? The O.T. is not only a record of the Hebrew people and their discovery of great religious truths but also a collection of the finest literature of the entire Near East. The O.T. is Hebrew literature, but it is more than that. It is the finest of the literature not only of the Hebrews but of the neighboring nations as well. The Hebrews lived among nations who influenced them greatly. The neighbors were usually in many respects culturally superior to the Hebrews, but the Hebrews led in religious discovery. But while the great leaders of Israel surpassed in religious insight and in understanding of God, they expressed their truths in forms which made use of the writings and traditions of other peoples. In our Bible, therefore, God is speaking to us through the experiences of multitudes of men—experiences ranging over thousands of years, in many different lands, and under many different cultures. The result is that the Bible is not the product of one man, nor of one people, but it is the best of literature and religious experience from countless peoples, in many lands, during untold ages of time. The purpose of the Bible is not to record history nor to unfold history, but to tell of God-guided men in history. Religion is vitally alive. It is not dictated, it is experienced; and our Bible is the world's greatest book of religious testimony.

This *Reading* is a very human story of the delight of Joseph at the turn of events that brought his brothers under his power. Feel the tension that must have been in his mind between desire for revenge and concern for those he loved. At first, revenge seemed to predominate, and Joseph had his brothers thrown into jail for three days.

Reading 24: Genesis 42:18–43:15

Joseph suddenly changed the plans. He would not get to see his father or brother by keeping the others in jail. His vengeance not only punished his brothers but also prevented Joseph from enjoying the thing he wanted most. So Simeon was kept as hostage and the others were freed. The condition of his release was that Benjamin should be brought on the next trip. Jacob was greatly alarmed by their reports and refused to let Benjamin accompany them. The discovery of the money alarmed the whole family. Just when it was discovered is not certain (cf. 42:28 and 42:35, and read *ABC,* p. 245). Coins were not yet in existence, but marked pieces of gold and silver were used in trade. Read the article entitled "Money" in *ABC,* p. 78.

Joseph attributed his changed attitude to his belief in God. Jacob likewise (43:14) prayed God's blessing upon his sons as he finally consented to their taking Benjamin. An important characteristic of Oriental people is the significant place that religion has in their lives. Religion is to them a vital part of everyday life, not something that is formal, to be put on and off with Sunday clothes. In every act they sought God's guidance and blessing. A journey was undertaken only with God's consent and protection. Is there danger in our modern world, with our stress upon the orderliness of the universe, that we shall lose our sense of dependence upon divine power? Religion becomes a formality to be observed, a meeting to be attended, rather than a way of life. Similarly, an individual who has an assured income, a comfortable living, a respected place in the community, an insurance program to care for the emergencies of sickness and death, is in danger of being smugly self-satisfied. He is the most difficult man for the minister to reach. List in your notebook the things for which men in Jacob's day would pray, and those for which men today—in the country or in the city—might pray. Now consider which of these prayers are made under the conviction that God is the magical source of things we otherwise cannot get, and which prayers recognize God as the source of all life and goodness, without whom we cannot live the noblest lives. Does your analysis suggest a method of approach to the self-satisfied individual who believes that he has all that life has to offer him?

At their father's suggestion, Joseph's brothers took double the purchase price on this second trip, and gifts of the country's best products in addition. Is there an essential difference between believing that "honesty is the best policy" and the conviction that honesty is a basic moral principle? Which of these attitudes is portrayed in this story?

Reading 25: Genesis 43:16-34

Two things strive for the center of interest in this *Reading*. The first is the great love expressed by Joseph for Benjamin. This was the reason for the great honor shown to the brothers in the feast and the reception at Joseph's house. There is a great contrast portrayed between the fear of the brothers and the magnanimity of Joseph.

The other center of interest is the social cleavage between Egyptians and Hebrews. They were served at separate tables. Joseph, now completely Egyptianized, remained at a different table from that of his brothers, as social custom demanded. Without doubt this phase of the story reflects custom that had a later development, and as the years passed became far worse. The separation between national groups began in an early day and has plagued mankind since. Tragically enough, the separation began, so far as we can tell, on religious grounds, and only later became nationalistic. A modern parallel may be found in the Protestant Church, where the sacraments are too often made the basis of division rather than of unification. The Egyptians and the Semites had different habits of eating, some arising out of their religious practices. The Christian of today cannot sit down to eat with his Jewish friend if that friend is an orthodox Jew. The Jews' religious laws make it impossible, and it is a courageous man who will dare to risk the social ostracism of his own group. As Christians we need to be aware of the social and religious customs that bind us and our non-Christian friends. We must be willing to surrender any practice, not involving principle, that divides mankind. Likewise we must recognize that another man's practices are his own and he alone has the right to modify or surrender them. We dare not force others to accept our ways of thinking and then call that Christianity. Christianity has always spread most effectively when the method of example and invitation has been used.

There is always a way of escape from the enslavement of custom. Joseph could not eat with his brothers, but he could carry portions from his table to theirs and so become the gracious host, unfettered by convention.

Written Work.—Write a brief sermon to preach to a group of men, on the topic "Religion Is Living with God." Bring out what it means to live with God and what such life does for men.

Reading 26: Genesis 44:1–45:15

Joseph was not yet ready to unmask himself. The brothers started for home, but were overtaken and arrested because of the disappearance of Joseph's cup. Just what Joseph's plan was is not quite clear, except that he had no intention of letting the brothers get home without knowing who he was. The cup hidden in Benjamin's sack had a dual use. It was a drinking cup, but was used also for divination. Joseph began his career with the Egyptians as a magician, and apparently he maintained the practice of magic. The ancient Egyptians used cups in which were dropped flakes of gold and silver, chips of gems, each having cryptic signs. Under the influence of the right incantation the divine powers were thought to arrange the pieces for answers. The modern practice of reading tea leaves is an offshoot. There are some who would defend fortunetelling by pointing out that it was believed in by the heroes of the Bible, therefore it must be right. What is wrong with that argument?

Judah's defense and plea for Benjamin is one of the outstanding passages in the Pentateuch. It was Judah who had placed Joseph in the pit and so saved his life. Perhaps it was this recollection that caused Joseph to break down and reveal himself to his brothers.

There were many things that prevented the brothers from recognizing Joseph. Because nothing had been heard of him since he had been sold into slavery, they assumed that he was dead. Even admitting that he might be alive, they scarcely expected to see a former slave in Joseph's position. Then there was the barrier of language and the difference of clothing. In addition, Joseph probably wore a false beard and the special headdress for his position in the official family of Pharaoh. Is it likely that there would have been reconciliation between Joseph and his brothers unless Joseph had taken the responsibility of making himself known? Probably not. It is frequently true that the wronged or offended individual is faced with the same problem that faced Joseph. Yet how many content themselves by saying: "He wronged me. It's up to him to make things right."

Reading 27: Genesis 45:16–46:7

The emphasis begins to shift now from the family to the tribes, for here is the beginning of the great tradition of bondage and deliverance from Egypt. These verses are by a writer who looks back over the long history of his people. One factor perhaps more than any other made Israel conscious of her destiny. That was the conviction that she was God-guided. This belief was not strong until in the time of the monarchy, but as the Israelites looked back upon history they were convinced that God had led them constantly.

Joseph knew his brothers well, for he charged them (v. 24) not to quarrel on the way back home. He knew that the coming of Jacob to Egypt and the salvation of the entire family from starvation depended upon the whole group's ability to work together in harmony. A quarrel could easily develop concerning the many gifts that had been showered upon them, and they would forget the greater task that lay ahead of them—that of getting their families moved to Egypt. How important was this ability of Joseph to understand the nature of those around him? Was this the key to his success as a leader? That man is fortunate who is deeply sensitive to the feelings of others and can sympathize with them, provided he keeps his own emotional balance and then guides his friends to deepened experiences. Joseph made provision for his brothers after full consideration of their needs and their emotions.

What did it cost Jacob to leave Palestine? Did he have strong ties with the country or was he a wanderer with no particular place of settlement? He was a tent dweller and had no "real estate" to sell. All his property was movable, which fact indicates that the tribes frequently shifted their home. In any case it was a long, hard journey from upper Palestine, probably near the valley of Jezreel, to Egypt. The cattle made the journey still more difficult. There is little wonder that, having arrived in Egypt and settled comfortably, there would be little desire to return to Palestine.

Reading 28: Genesis 46:26–47:27

Read "The Chronology of the O.T.," *ABC*, p. 108f. We must place the migration of the Jacob family into Egypt near 1600 B.C. A total of only seventy people is listed in the group, and historians can scarcely hope that so small a number will be noted in any of the Egyptian writings. The only information we have about them is in the Bible. They are remembered for two reasons: God delivered their descendants from slavery in Egypt, and from those descendants came the great religious leadership of the nation Israel. Later Hebrews believed that the great patriarchs—Abraham, Isaac, and Jacob—knew that they were to be the ancestors of a great people. Throughout the stories connected with their lives runs the sense of responsibility that these men had for their families. The old tribal system of the desert placed upon the husband of the family the responsibility of providing not only food but also religious leadership. When the later prophets cried out for a return to the ideals of the desert, they most of all desired that the men of Israel

53

would recover their sense of moral and spiritual leadership in their families.

The immediate danger that faced the family of Jacob as they came to Egypt was that his sons would be given favored places in the official family of Pharaoh. Jacob, and Joseph, wanted them to remain shepherds (see *ABC*, p. 246).

V. 22 in ch. 47 indicates that the religion of Egypt was officially supported. Not only were the priests exempt from taxation, but their support came from Pharaoh. Did this make it easier or harder for them to make moral decisions? Could they make unbiased judgment of Pharaoh or his government? Egyptian religion was primarily the observance of ritual and not the making of moral pronouncements. Would this make any difference?

Vv. 23-24 explain the origin of the Egyptian practice of taking one fifth of all produce as a national tax (see *ABC*, p. 246). This heavy taxation by the state of Egypt, and by the Temple in Babylon, finally bankrupted the countries. Perhaps it was placed in the Hebrew Scripture for a warning to Israel.

Reading 29: Genesis 47:28–49:28

As stated before, the blessing by a father was of extreme importance in Bible times. It could be given only once and was considered to have a determining influence forever afterward upon the one blessed. The thought seems to have been that a man was permitted to come once to God and ask a special benediction upon his successor and his family. If you could pray *once* for your son as he left to establish his own home, what would you include in that prayer? Confronted with this responsibility, the fathers in Israel gave long and serious consideration to it. Many of these blessings have been remembered in verse. There are two possible explanations of this. Either the framer of the blessing took the trouble to put the blessing into poetical form so that later generations would more easily remember it, or a later generation versified the blessing as an aid to memory. In either case, the result is the same. It was thought important to remember the prayers of blessing of one's ancestors. It is probable, too, that constant remembrance of the blessings stimulated men to achieve the ideal set for them in the prayer of blessing.

There are two accounts of blessing by Jacob (Gen. 48: 12-20 and 49:2-27). The first transfers the blessing that belonged to Joseph to the grandsons Ephraim and Manasseh. The story is told at a later date to account for the presence of the tribes of that name in the list of the Twelve Tribes and for the absence of the Joseph tribe. There is emphasis also upon the superiority of Ephraim to Manasseh.

The blessing in 49:2f. is a listing of the tribes of Israel and their recognized virtues and failures. The poem comes from the time of the monarchy. In this case, Joseph is listed and Ephraim and Manasseh are omitted. There is no mention of residence in Egypt. The whole atmosphere is far removed from that of the preceding chapter. Both stories, however, keep the emphasis upon the importance of the father's blessing. For detailed comment read *ABC*, p. 247.

Reading 30: Genesis 49:29–50:26

The deaths of Jacob and Joseph close this section of the Law. In the stories there is an intermixture of Egyptian and Hebrew custom. The bodies of both men were embalmed in Egyptian fashion. At Jacob's request his body was taken to the cave at Machpelah so that he would rest with his ancestors. Joseph's body was placed in a coffin, as was the custom for leading Egyptians; but Joseph had requested that whenever the Israelites should return to Palestine the coffin should be taken along. It is difficult to separate the original stories from later accretions, but there are some contrasts worth noting.

The careful preparation of the body of a deceased person took "forty days." Egyptians believed in a life beyond the grave in which the body would be necessary, hence they took many precautions to protect and preserve the body. In the process of mummification, the viscera and the brain were removed from the body. But the heart was replaced after treatment. The heart of the deceased was needed at the time of judgment, for it was weighed against the feather of truth. If the deceased had done no wrong, then he was lighthearted and could pass the judgment test. Presumably the Egyptian needed no brain in the new life; but that is understandable, for to him the heart was the seat of emotion and intelligence.

Jacob and Joseph did not accept the Egyptian beliefs but simply allowed their survivors to follow the generally accepted practice. It was another case of a practice that once had had religious importance now being simply a matter of social acceptance. How many funeral practices of today have lost their significance and are followed simply because few care to deviate from old patterns! The Hebrew also believed that eternal life belonged to the race, not the individual. It was therefore essential to have offspring, and it was necessary to give that offspring a good start by seeing that it inherited a good name. Hebrew morals have constantly been strengthened because of a deep sense of responsibility to posterity. Modern men can still be challenged at that point.

When the Law was first compiled there were no divisions, and therefore no headings of "Genesis" and so on. Because of the limitations imposed by writing materials it became necessary to make a divsion into "books." Five divisions were made, and the Hebrews referred to "the five fifths of the Law." Later, names were added to the books, the opening word or phrase of each division still being the Hebrew name for that particular book. The present names come to us from the titles given to each book in the Greek translation of the O. T. Yet there is particular significance in the title "Genesis," for it is an introduction to the story of the Hebrews as a nation.

Written Work.—Write a statement of 500 to 1000 words about the great religious teachings of the book of Genesis: truths about God and man, the right way of life, and man's need for religious instruction.

IV

FROM SLAVERY TO SINAI
Exodus 1:1–18:27

THE book of Exodus is concerned primarily with the story of Moses, the Great Lawgiver and the Deliverer of Israel. After a brief introduction (1:1-22) the story of Moses begins. Only ten verses are devoted to his birth and childhood, the rest of the book being given to his lifework. He seldom leaves the scene of action, and though he may temporarily be absent from the front of the stage his influence is always strongly present. The phrase "The Lord said unto Moses" is repeated with monotonous regularity every few verses. The book is about Moses, not by Moses. Read *ABC,* pp. 134f., 249-51.

The importance of Moses is seen in the large place that has been given to him in Hebrew tradition. He is credited with having led the whole nation from Egyptian slavery, bringing them to the border of their new home country, revealing their God to them, establishing the Covenant between God and the people, giving the Law to Israel; and late Jewish tradition insisted that he had written the complete Pentateuch. Other writings have been credited to him, but we need not be concerned here with that problem. The key to the greatness of the life of Moses is his religious leadership. We shall see the amazing growth that he made as a leader, and the corresponding growth in his religious knowledge.

There are many problems connected with the study of the life of Moses. He has been so highly honored by later generations that it is difficult to separate fact from glorification. Because of the confusion of early Hebrew traditions, it is almost impossible to fix with certainty the time in which Moses lived. There is greater evidence for the twelfth century B.C. than for any other period, though there are those who date Moses in the fourteenth century.

There is increasing evidence that he led the tribe of Levi and not the Twelve Tribes of Israel. The greatness of Moses rests not in the size of the group that he led but rather in the kind of leadership he gave and the teachings he bequeathed to posterity through them. The Bible puts its emphasis upon Moses the lawgiver rather than upon Moses as liberator. We shall discover that the Hebrew writers were keen in their judgments.

Reading 31: Exodus 1:1–2:10

After a brief summary or repetition of Gen. 46, this new section immediately gives the setting necessary for an understanding of the condition of slavery in Egypt. A new king was upon the throne, one who knew nothing of Joseph. The Bible does not give the name of this Pharaoh, and scholars disagree about which Pharaoh was responsible for the oppression. We can only guess. Our writer simply indicates that conditions had completely changed since Joseph's times. How long this condition had lasted is not stated, nor do we know how many years had elapsed since the death of Joseph. Our historical curiosity might be satisfied if we could identify the Pharaoh of the oppression, but it is doubtful that this would give us more religious insight. Hard bondage and the slaughter of male children are illustrations of the difficult conditions under which the Hebrews lived. Our writer is insisting that God never forsook them.

Parallel stories from Babylon and Egypt of the use of "an ark of bulrushes" (see *ABC*, p. 253a) neither confirm nor deny the truth of the story of Moses. We simply know from these other stories that such boats did exist in those days. The interest of the early Hebrews centered in the way in which Jochebed outwitted the Egyptians. How they must have delighted in the story of this mother being hired to nurse her own child and paid by the very enemy she had determined to outwit. We have here also a possible clue to the later career of Moses. In that part of the world, even today, children are breast fed far longer than in Europe or America. Scarcity of other suitable food is the major reason for this. Is it possible, then, that Moses stayed with his mother long enough to become acquainted with some of the ancient traditions of his own people? In any case, there seems to be a mixture of Hebrew and Egyptian "education" in his life.

His name is now generally admitted to be Egyptian, a name meaning "son." Several of the Pharaohs have this same name as a part of theirs: Thut-moses, Ah-moses. Later writers naturally sought the meaning of the name "Moses" in their own language, and called him "the one drawn out," forgetting that an Egyptian princess would not be likely to speak Hebrew. Our writers were not concerned with historical accuracies. Their concern was to relate the story of their nation with emphasis upon the guidance of God in history.

How much was Moses indebted to his mother for a knowledge of the customs and traditions of his people? If Moses had been educated purely in the Egyptian pattern of living, how did he know that he was related to the Semitic slaves of the Egyptians? Did Moses learn first of the God of the Hebrews from Jochebed his mother? How important are the early years of childhood for religious development? Moses learned much, later on, from such men as Jethro, whose daughter he married; but he had no sympathy with the Egyptian religion. Is this because of his loyalty to his own people and their traditions? Write in your notebook the influences that came into the early life of Moses.

Reading 32: Exodus 2:11–3:15

There were a number of influences that entered into what is usually referred to as "the call of Moses." There was first of all his reaction to the suffering of his people and a desire to defend them. This led to his killing an Egyptian.

After fleeing to Midian he came under the influence of a Midianite priest whose name is not quite clear. It is given as Reuel in 2:18 and as Jethro in 3:1. Here is another indication of differences in the Hebrew traditions. If Moses had written these two chapters he would certainly have given the name of his father-in-law correctly in each case (see *ABC*, p. 254*a*). Still another influence was that of the burning bush. Many attempts have been made to explain this event. We must confess that we are too far away from the event and have too scanty information to make an intelligent judgment, but it is clear that out there in the desert Moses became conscious of the presence of God. There came to Moses the conviction that he must be the agent of God in the liberation of the Hebrew people from slavery in Egypt. The "call" came to Moses as it must come to all men. He became conscious of the need of others, that God was the answer to their need, and that he could be the agent of God in answering that need. Preparation and training are usually necessary before a man can adequately function as the agent of God, and that is a part of the cost of response. Moses' first answer was that he was not prepared to be the liberator of his people. Why is it that men are more humble about their capabilities in the work of religion than in politics, business, or industry? Is it true humility or an unconscious fear of failure?

Two things need to be noted in connection with v. 14. (For a discussion of the meaning of the name of God, see *ABC*, p. 256.) First, the people to whom Moses was sent needed to be convinced that God could deliver them; and, second, they were much more likely to respond to Moses' appeal if they already knew the God in whose name he spoke. He must have made an appeal in the name of the God of the ancestors Abraham, Isaac, and Jacob. This is the significance of v. 15. We no longer know how the name was pronounced, but it did have a familiar sound to the Hebrew slaves, and when they heard the name it carried the conviction that God would be able to accomplish their liberation. Finally Moses came to the realization that when

God challenges a man to a task God is with him. Man may fail God, but God will not fail man.

Reading 33: Exodus 3:16–4:17

Magic plays a great part in the religious history of man. Even today men are not free of it. The contest recorded here was a matching of wits. All through the ancient East the ability to do magic was the great proof that a man had special power from God and therefore could be heard as God's spokesman. This is why so much attention is given to the miraculous in many ancient writings. Under the influence of the teachings of the prophets and the message of Christianity emphasis has shifted to the moral content of a man's message, but occasionally there is a group that looks for proof by the miraculous. Which is more important, to have a message with high moral significance, or to be able to pick up a venomous snake without being bitten? Which will be likely to influence men to strive for higher levels of living?

Emphasis upon the cleverness of the Hebrews, rather than upon their morality, is seen in 3:18 and 3:22. Since their God was considered a resident of the desert, it was quite natural for them to ask permission to journey into the desert for communion or feasting with that God. Apparently Pharaoh realized that with the Hebrews gone three days into the desert the chances of their returning to Egypt would be slim. The appeal of Moses failed; and when Pharaoh finally did give permission it was because of his fear of further punishment, not his desire to permit the Hebrews to worship in the desert. Further cleverness is evidenced by the plan to "spoil" Egypt. It was planned to borrow expensive things from the Egyptians and then to decamp with them. Gifts would be of no significance; for custom demanded that, when a gift was accepted, one of similar value should be given to the donor. In the case of an exchange there would be no gain to the Hebrews. In that day, the morals of the tribe applied only within the tribe and not in relation to other tribes or groups of people.

61

Chs. 3 and 4 list a number of excuses made by Moses (3:11, 13; 4:1). Moses' last excuse was that he had no ability as a speaker. The selection of Aaron as spokesman solved the problem, and to Moses was left the responsibility of the content of the messages. In 7:1 Aaron is called the "prophet" of Moses. A prophet was one who spoke on behalf of another, usually speaking for God. In 4:16 he is called simply a "mouth" to Moses. Again the emphasis is made that whenever a man responds wholeheartedly and sincerely to God's call to a certain task, no obstacles are insurmountable.

Reading 34: Exodus 4:18–5:19

The driving foremen in 5:10f. are well pictured. They must meet a quota and neither shortage of materials nor shortage of help must deflect them from that goal. Human life was very cheap in that day; it is difficult for us to imagine the inhumanity that was displayed. The sightseer of Egypt's wonders should pause to remember the blood, toil, tears, and sweat that have gone into those monuments to man's insatiable conceit. The statue of fame sometimes rests on the writhing bodies of broken slaves.

In 5:1-11 is another interesting study in human reactions. Pharaoh, when confronted with the request to make a three-day religious journey, stated that the people were not working hard enough. Note that the request by Moses was for a religious holiday, not for relief from suffering and hardship. Why did Moses ask for a holiday instead of a correction of working conditions? Was he afraid? Remember, his mission was to gain complete freedom for the people, not better conditions. He does not seem to have been afraid, and he refused to be turned aside from his main purpose. Pharaoh, on the other hand, believed that if he made working conditions more difficult the people would have less time to think about their problems, and in addition would probably turn against their champion, Moses. These are problems that still face reformers and their followers. Many movements have been completely abandoned because in the first steps to get improved conditions things were made temporarily worse. Does it mean that people are essentially selfish, or are they afraid that sacrificed values and pleasures will never be restored? Compare this attitude with the wise man's statement "Where there is no vision, the people perish" (Prov. 29:18—A.V.).

The refusal of the Egyptian taskmasters to give straw to the Hebrews while demanding the same number of bricks was completely unfair. Straw was necessary to bind the clay together and make it easier to work and more durable. The Hebrews were not concerned about the durability, but they did know that without straw their job was infinitely harder. They must supply their own substitute for straw, so they searched the fields for stubble. That in turn meant less time for making the same number of bricks. It was not a question of "bricks without straw," but of providing their own binder straw. The whole purpose of Pharaoh's decision was to make the Hebrews work harder and longer.

Reading 35: Exodus 5:20–6:13; 6:28–7:24

The change in religious thinking is shown by the different writers who are quoted in chs. 5 to 11, samples of which are given in this reading. The oldest writer, known as "J," wrote about the middle of the ninth century B.C. He lists seven plagues, and he portrays Moses as the one who told Pharaoh in advance that these plagues would be sent by God. About one hundred years later, the "E" writer tells his version of the plagues. He lists only five of them, and in this picture Moses is the one responsible for the plagues. He produces them instantly by means of his magic rod. Here the emphasis is upon Moses the magician, with Pharaoh giving concessions for each magical act. The final writer, known as "P," groups these stories together, with the result that there are ten plagues listed and Moses is a combination of foreteller and magician.

Suggestions have been made that the series of plagues was a series of natural events related to the flooding of the Nile, and that these plagues came with irritating regularity

63

to the Nile Valley. If that had been true, then there would have been no value in them for Moses' purpose. No Pharaoh could be persuaded that a Hebrew God was responsible for plagues, no matter how severe, if those same plagues had been known frequently in Egyptian history, particularly within the memory of those living. The force of the account is that something unknown and startling was being visited upon Pharaoh and his people. Note further that the people in that day could not be expected to know the God of all nature. They identified certain processes of nature with specific gods, but it was many centuries before mankind came to know that one God was responsible for all acts of nature. Even then, it was the Hebrews who led the way to that faith. The Egyptians remained believers in many gods until their acceptance of Mohammedanism. The insistence of these chapters is that it was very difficult for the Hebrews to escape from Egypt and that their final deliverance was possible only through the leadership of Moses and the guidance of God.

Written Work.—Outline the steps by which Moses became the leader in the liberation of the Hebrews. Be careful to list all the influences for or against his decision to accept the challenge.

Reading 36: Exodus 12:1-28; 12:43–13:16

There is a close parallel between the American custom of Thanksgiving and the Hebrew Passover. Both are family feasts commemorating deliverance by God. Both express thanks for divine blessings. There are a number of differences, however. The Hebrew feast, because it is a dramatization, is usually eaten in haste; and the American meal is one of leisure. The Hebrew feast must always be eaten after nightfall. There is no restriction on American custom. The Hebrew meal has many firmly fixed religious customs which may not be violated, but the American Thanksgiving assumes that participants will offer their appropriate thanks, each after his own manner. We shall fail to understand the significance of the Passover for the Hebrew unless we see that the emphasis in this celebration is on thanksgiving to God for his preservation of them as a nation.

In this celebration, as in other religious rites of the Hebrews, specific instructions are given to the father for conducting it, and provision is made for religious instruction. When the child asks, "Father, what is the meaning of all this?" the father has an answer ready at hand, (see Ex. 13:14). In practice, the son is expected always to ask the question and the father always to answer. In some respects the instruction becomes mechanical. But always the children are being reminded of the foundations of their religion and its practices. The observance of this ceremony has always remained in the home, and the father is the priest of the family.

Read *ABC*, pp. 262f., for an account of the possible origin of the Feast of the Passover. Here is another example of Moses' appeal through familiar patterns. The feast had been neglected and perhaps forgotten by many of the people in slavery. Now Moses revived the custom and gave it new religious significance based upon the recent experiences of the people. Changes were constantly made in the religion of Israel because the Hebrews had new religious experiences. Sometimes they moved to higher levels of conduct, sometimes they descended to lower levels. In this instance they moved from superstitious dread toward a higher thought of God. At the time of the revival of this ceremony by Moses, all those in the community participated in it. They were part of the community, and they all experienced the excitement of escape from Egypt. Later, the Feast of the Passover was restricted to those who were circumcised Hebrews (Ex. 12:43f.). Foreigners were forbidden. Intense nationalism tended to make the Hebrews exclusive people, and was one of the causes of persecution. Religious customs change in the light of new experiences. Old patterns take on new meanings. They may become better or worse. There are good and bad changes in the celebration of the Feast of the Passover.

65

Reading 37: Exodus 14:1–15:21

Nothing in Egyptian literature gives even a hint of the destruction of Pharaoh's officers or part of his army. Nothing in Hebrew history is celebrated more constantly than this deliverance from Egypt and the host of Pharaoh. In several of the psalms (78, 106, 136) and throughout Hebrew literature there is frequent reference to the deliverance. We can understand why the Egyptians have not recorded the event. The ancients never recorded defeats, and only occasionally do they admit of "strategic withdrawals." And, too, since the number of Hebrews was relatively small, the army contingent assigned to pursue them would be correspondingly small. The loss of a small group of officers and men in pursuit of desert fugitives would hardly be engraved upon Egyptian monuments.

Several things stand out in the minds of later Hebrews. First, they saw the hand of God in the history of their ancestors. This was a great victory for the Hebrew God over the gods of Egypt. Next, they saw in the deliverance God's approval of Moses. He was a great leader appointed of God. The Hebrews also stressed the complete defeat of the Egyptians. In that day Egypt was a great power; and throughout the history of the Hebrews, Egypt was a power of great importance. Constantly in Hebrew literature there is reflected the bitter distrust and hatred of this great power. In a day when many political leaders would trust in military power and political alliance there were those who said: "Some trust in chariots, and some in horses; but we will remember the name of the Lord" (Psa. 20:7—A.V.). Finally, the Hebrew remembered that through this deliverance he obtained freedom; and the stress was upon the completeness of the freedom, not upon the number delivered. The Hebrew writer was realistic enough to remember that even in the success of the flight from Egypt there were those who cried and complained and thought that their former condition of slavery was preferable.

God's answer to Moses in 14:15-16 insists not only upon

action on the part of the people but also that Moses is perfectly capable of handling this emergency. Like many since his day, Moses was inclined to resort to prayer at the least sign of trouble and to believe that through prayer God would somehow miraculously solve all his problems. There is real insight in these verses, which say in effect: "Moses, the answer to this problem is in the kind of leadership you give to this people." It was necessary for the people to go forward, but to go forward under intelligent leadership and purpose. Many religious groups have assumed that a lot of activity, usually physical, is the label of a good program. What should be the standards by which we judge any problem? Is it wise to start on any program until we have defined our goals and mapped out the road over which we must travel to attain the goals? Did Moses discover that it was needful not only to plan carefully but also to gain the confidence of his followers? Could his bid for freedom have been successful if he had failed to gain such confidence?

Reading 38: Exodus 15:22–16:36

The latter part of ch. 15 and the next three chapters deal largely with two problems. First, there are listed the stopping places of the Israelites. Most of these places are now unknown; and though many attempts have been made to identify them, we still have no satisfactory solution to the problem of the route of the escaping Israelites. It is generally agreed among recent scholars that the journeys of the Israelites were in the plains south and southwest of Palestine. Certainly Moses, who had lived for many years in the plains of Midian and was well acquainted with the roads and caravan routes to Palestine, would not have made the mistake of journeying south into the Sinai Peninsula. In any case, we must confess that the names of the stopping places were remembered only hazily by the later writers. But the Hebrew writer was never confused about the ultimate goal. From his point of view it was far more important to remember the goal and the determination of the people to reach it than it was to identify halfway marks. In America we have emphasized details of journeys, and it has been the custom for historical societies to place monuments to mark out the trails of the covered wagons, to place bronze tablets "where Washington slept," and the like. Which is more important, to remember that a group of Pilgrims came to this country seeking religious freedom, or to know the exact spot on the Atlantic Seaboard where they landed? It may be possible and highly desirable to know both, but there is sometimes the danger that our curiosity for historical detail may be substituted for the search for religious and intellectual development.

The second problem with which the writer was concerned was that of man's need and God's care. Many attempts have been made to explain the quail and manna as accidents or manifestations of nature. Remember that the ancient writer was writing for the ancients and not for the modern mind. They and he believed that God was the Lord of nature and that he could do what he would. Our more modern approach has been to insist that God works through natural law; but at times we have imprisoned God within the laws of the universe, and sometimes have lost him in the processes of nature. The ideas of the ancient Hebrew writer were very simple. He knew nothing of modern scientific knowledge, but he did stress the fact that God had a concern for his people and left nothing undone to help and guide them to their ultimate destiny. His religious conviction was voiced in terms of and in harmony with the scientific knowledge of his day. Newer knowledge should give us better understanding of God, his purposes, and how he works. Modern minds may find difficulties in the stories of the quail and manna, but remember that these were ways by which the Hebrew expressed his belief in God who cares for his people. Faith and knowledge are friends, but faith and ignorance are enemies.

Reading 39: Exodus 18:1-27

Ch. 18 tells a beautiful story of a father-in-law's advice. Jethro rejoiced to see Moses and his daughter Zipporah again. He expressed his conviction that the God of the Hebrews had triumphed over the gods of Egypt. He led Moses, Aaron, and the elders of Israel in a religious sacrifice, the purpose of which most probably was to express thanks to God for deliverance. On the following day he watched Moses carefully in his administrative and judicial duties. Then Jethro gave advice skillfully but forcefully. Note how he led Moses into a receptive mood by his questions. He did not criticize Moses or his skill in handling cases, but he made the suggestion that Moses would not be able to keep up the grueling pace and in the end the people would suffer the loss of their leader. His suggestion was simply that Moses should delegate responsibility to capable leaders. It is worth noting that Jethro flattered Moses by suggesting that Moses should remain the highest court of appeal. But Jethro was doing more than flattering Moses; he was keeping the law of the desert. Even today, the lowliest Arab has the privilege of coming into the presence of the highest ruler and pleading his case if he feels that justice has not been given him by lower judges. The Oriental monarch is always ex officio chief justice of the supreme court. There is a curious mingling of the despotism of the ruling caste and the inviolable right to justice for every man.

The charactersitics suggested for the chosen leaders are worth noting. They will apply whether we are choosing church leaders or political representatives. One preacher used this chapter for the lesson on the Sunday preceding a national election. He made his reading of the lesson doubly effective by prefacing the reading with a carefully worded introduction on the permanent significance of the characteristics needed for leadership. Jethro said the leaders must be (1) capable, (2) God-fearing, (3) honest, and (4) opposed to unjust gain. Jethro did not say, "Call for volunteers." Too many good programs have been ruined by volunteer leadership. For a big job men must be selected carefully. Often in volunteer leadership we have all the qualities needed except the first, namely, capability. Jethro put that first. Politics permits men to volunteer to run for office, but the final choice rests upon the vote of the people. It combines the values of willing and capable leadership. But even politicians recognize that at times it is needful to draft capable leadership. Every pastor discovers that, soon or late in his ministry; the wise pastor discovers it early. Leaders should also be God-fearing and honest. What would happen if Christians should insist that their political representatives should have these two characteristics? If they are to be representative, should they not have them? Finally, Jethro said that leaders should be haters of unjust gain. Not only should they have high standards for themselves, but they should be opposed to low standards in other—and should be outspoken about it. The last suggestion of Jethro was that their responsibilities should be divided up in such a way as to give Moses complete supervision over the people and a control of the work of these leaders.

Written Work.—Write an essay describing the indebtedness of Moses to Jethro (a) socially, (b) religiously, and (c) politically.

V

LAWS OF GOD AND MAN
Exodus 19:1–40:38

A CAREFUL examination of the law of any community or people will reflect the stages of development in that community. One can pick out those laws that were passed in the "horse and buggy" days. Then come newer laws that control the speed and operation of automobiles. Now we are adding laws to regulate radio and air traffic. Law is formulated always in answer to need for it. Some legislation may be forward looking, but no legislators pass laws several hundreds of years in advance of social conditions. This was true in ancient Israel. The people who lived in the desert did not make housing laws for city dwellings. This is one of the many ways by which scholars have been able to date the laws of Israel. For a summary of the development of Hebrew Law read Jordan, *ABC*, pp. 145f.

One of the outstanding contributions of careful scholarship is the knowledge we now have of the moral development of the Hebrews as reflected in their Books of Law. Law reflects moral thinking, and this is truer of the Hebrews than of any Western people because the Hebrew thought that the only law worthy of consideration was that which came from God. The Hebrew made little or no distinction between the secular and the religious. He was conscious of God in all phases of life. He did not think of law as the product of the court or rulers, and religion as a matter to be associated only with the Temple. Law and religion were definitely partners in his world. And as he followed the teachings of the prophets and climbed to higher levels of moral thinking, his law climbed also. He applied in law what he had discovered in religion. Indeed, he could not make a separation.

In this section of our study of the Law we begin the Law proper. Up to now we have been reading tradition and history. Now there will be little of history and much of law. All law, in a later day, was attributed to Moses, but actually it came from many nations and various times. In general, we may say that the remainder of Exodus includes law from Moses, the law already in Canaan, Babylonian and Assyrian law, and, possibly, some Hittite law. The books of Numbers and Leviticus give us the latest form of law in Israel as written down by the priests after the Babylonian exile. Much of what they wrote was ancient tradition from as early as the days of Moses, but some of it was law formulated to regulate the nation in its later days. The book of Deuteronomy, for example, which reflects the influence of the teachings of the great prophets of the eighth century B.C., is one of the most important sections of Hebrew Law. Not all the law is contained in the Books of the Law. In one outstanding instance law appears in a book of prophecy, chs. 40-48 of Ezekiel (see *The Prophets,* the third book of this course in the O.T.). The Hebrews believed that religion should regulate the whole of life, and the teachings of their great religious leaders usually found expression in the Law of Israel. Here lies the explanation of why the heart of Hebrew Law has become basic to the law of the entire civilized world; it is law based upon moral conviction.

Reading 40: Exodus 20:1-17

One of the most significant contributions ever made to law is found in this chapter. The Ten Commandments have become the foundation upon which the moral law of many nations has been built. Read *ABC,* pp. 268b-69. The Ten Commandments may be divided into two sections: the first five deal with religion as it centers around God and the home; the last five treat of man's relation to his fellow man. It has been pointed out that the commandments are almost completely negative, yet it should be observed that there are things that a man with positive convictions cannot do. That does not mean that his outlook is negative, simply that there are certain things that he will not permit himself to do.

The first commandment puts loyalty to the God of the Hebrews first. They believed that there were separate gods for separate nations; it was only later that they were led by the prophets to discover that there is but one God. The loyalty demanded by this commandment was necessary, for it involved loyalty to the central fact of religious conviction.

The second commandment prohibits the use of idols. The Hebrews were surrounded then and later by people who worshiped idols. See Isa. 44:9-20; Jer. 10:1-5; Ezek. 8: 9-11. There is no attempt here to prohibit a picture, as some have supposed; the command is against worship by means of idols.

The third commandment prohibits the use of God's name for evil purposes. Do not ask God to curse a man, or to do evil to him. Read this in the *American Translation* and compare it with the A.V. Does the newer translation have any more meaning for you?

Observance of the Sabbath is commanded positively in the fourth commandment. Sabbath observance was not known before the time of Moses, and the development of the Sabbath as a day of rest and worship was the result of long development in the light of the teachings of the prophets. Compare v. 10 with Mk. 2:27-28. Why does Jesus make this statement?

Honor to parents has been one of the fundamentals of Jewish society. See Eph. 6:1; Col. 3:20. Note also that in Col. 3:21 Paul adds a word on the responsibility of parents. What is the relation of juvenile delinquency to these verses?

Commandments 6-9 deal with crimes against persons. Religion is right relation not only with God but with one's fellows. At first these commands applied only within the tribe. Now we have extended them to all nations. Dare we

73

say that nations have moral responsibility? What does it mean to say that nations are guilty of theft or murder or false charges against their fellows?

The last commandment concerns covetousness. Note that the wife is listed with property. In this command as given in Deuteronomy the wife is listed first, then the home, then other property. Does this show any development in the place of woman in society? Compare Jesus' statement in Mt. 5:27-28. Was Jesus concerned here with literal observance of the Law, or with its moral content? Is it possible for us to keep these commandments and yet be unconcerned about the welfare of our fellows?

Reading 41: Exodus 21:1-11; 22:25-27; 23:1-9, 18-19

The Covenant Code is so called because of its association with the Covenant made at Sinai. Much of this code had its origin several hundred years earlier among the Babylonians. A comparison of the Hammurabi Code and the Covenant Code shows close parallels. Both codes are primarily civil, not religious, in character. There are some differences due to the long period of time intervening and to the changed economic values. In Babylon a man served only three years before being eligible for freedom. In Palestine he must serve six years. This same code may have served not only the Babylonians but also the Canaanites. In any case, we are forced to confess that this code is useful only for a settled agricultural community. It could not apply to desert life. It deals with farming and farm animals, with houses and lands, fields and vineyards, and offerings that only a farmer could be expected to bring to God.

There is a curious mixture of primitive religion and high moral content. This results from the many centuries of revision that have gone into this section. In Ex. 21:6 God is in the doorpost, and a covenant is made by putting an awl through the lobe of the servant's ear into the doorpost. The Babylonians and Assyrians had a similar belief. God in the doorpost was the guardian of the home or the temple.

74

Assyrians carved the doorpost to show that it was a god. A parallel teaching insisted that God was in the threshold, and the custom of carrying a bride across the threshold of her new home is a survival of this ancient belief. By contrast see the high level of thinking in 22:25-27. Men had little clothing in those days, and a man's outer clothing had to serve also as his bedcover. Therefore a garment taken in pledge for a debt and kept overnight would result in the owner's suffering from the cold night air. Be humane, says this law, and allow the man to use his coat for a bedcover if that is all he has.

Men have long followed the will of the majority, and that is the basis of democracy. But the law in 23:1-3 stresses the need for clear-thinking individuals and minorities.

The latter part of 23:19 prohibits boiling a live kid in its mother's milk. This is not merely a humanitarian provision. A few years ago an old ritual from north Syria was discovered, dating from the fourteenth century B.C. This particular ritual was written for the magical purpose of producing rain, and the most potent magic known to these ancients was that of boiling a newly born kid in its mother's milk. The law in 23:19 is an example of religious protest. This law says in effect: "We do not believe in such magical practices."

The close of ch. 23 reiterates the conviction of the Hebrews that God was their leader and that enemies would be driven out ahead of them. They were realistic enough to see that the way would not be easy.

Reading 42: Exodus 24

This chapter is an interruption of the account of Moses on Mount Sinai (see *ABC,* pp. 271f.), but it is an important chapter in Hebrew religion. This one chapter is made up of three different sources of tradition. Vv. 1-2, and 9-11 seem to be the oldest part, and these verses tell the story of Moses, three leaders, and seventy elders seeing the vision of God and eating a meal in his presence.

Such meals are among the oldest forms of sacrifice. According to the law of the desert there is a bond between men who have eaten together. Upon the host there is special responsibility for protecting those who have been his guests. In this meal, God was considered the host and therefore the protector of his guests. Read *ABC*, pp. 75f. The second account (24:3-8) is from the later source and deals with the blood covenant. Blood was sprinkled upon the altar, which represented the divine presence, and upon the people. Sprinkled with the same blood, the Deity and his people were now joined with an unbreakable bond. There is no mention of a vision, nor of the three leaders and seventy elders. An important contribution is added by this writer. The Covenant is portrayed as mutual agreement between the people and God's representative, Moses. V. 4 states that Moses wrote down the Law of God, and in v. 7 that Law is read to the people. Then the people accept the responsibility of obeying that Law. Only after this does Moses sprinkle them with blood, signifying the completion of the blood bond. In the Covenant there was responsibility on both sides. One of the failures of later Israel was that the people forgot their obligation. They assumed that since they were a chosen people therefore all would be well in the day of judgment. The ringing cry of the prophets was that the chosen people had assumed a responsibility of living according to the moral standards of God.

The remainder of the chapter, from the later Priestly writers, reads almost as an anti-climax. The people have already entered into religious covenant, but Moses is now portrayed as returning to the mountain to receive the God-written Law. These sentences are an introduction to the next seven chapters, which are almost completely a priestly record of the building and furnishing of the tabernacle, the robing of the priests, and the performance of the ritual of the tabernacle.

76

Reading 43: Exodus 25

This chapter is for many readers one of the less interesting chapters of the Bible because of its attention to details of building construction. The details are characteristic of much of the writing from the Priestly school. Church leaders in ancient times seem to have been great lovers of statistics. There are, however, some points worth noting in this and the following chapters. The priests reflected the thinking of many people and unconsciously glorified the past. The tabernacle portrayed here could never have existed in the desert, but the priests and people were sincere in believing that it had been there. One preacher, reporting to the district conference for his church, stated, "My church's future is all behind it." The glorification of the past often detracts from the opportunities of the present. One pastor's program was constantly defeated, because every proposal was answered with "In the good old days, we did it better and bigger." Finally, in desperation, the pastor checked the old records; and it was an amazed official board who saw in graphs and figures that the old days were not as good as reported. It would have been good for Israel if a more exact picture could have been given of desert worship (see *Reading* 45).

Nevertheless, the priests did remember the things that are essential for the building of God's sanctuary. First, it began with the people. An offering was taken, which was to be received only from those who expressed willingness to contribute. Gifts were to be made according to ability. There was no coinage in those days, and offerings had to be of materials available to the people. Much of it was material actually used in construction. Second, people and leaders recognized that it was sound procedure to set aside a place where man could worship God. The place was to be made worshipful by the presence of emblems to remind the worshiper of God's presence. Central in the Holy of Holies was the Ark which was to contain the Law. It became a permanent symbol of the Covenant and of the obligation assumed by the people to live by those laws. On the ark was a covering of gold, which symbolized the presence of God, who was thought to hover over the "mercy seat," or covering. At one side of the other room, known as the Holy Place, stood a table, and upon the table were the food and utensils for a meal. The meal was always there, probably representing permanently the Covenant meal. Opposite the table stood a seven-branched lampstand, beautifully made. Its design may have been influenced by Egypt. Its purpose was simply that of providing light, and it was only later that it carried symbolic significance. Between the two rooms was a curtain, or veil.

Symbols are useful provided we understand their significance. But the meanings of symbols change. In 25:19f. instructions are given for the placing of "cherubs." "Cherub" is an Assyrian name for the god of the doorpost (see *Reading* 41). In Assyrian times the doorpost was carved and the image was fourfold. It had a man's head, the wings of an eagle, the body of a bull, and the feet and tail of a lion. Later, the Jews thought of "cherubs" as angels. (In early Christian times, these four parts of the cherub were made symbols of the Gospels. That is a strange journey for a cherub, but it indicates how religion adapts old symbols to new meanings.)

Reading 44: Exodus 27

The altar was one of the most important articles of furniture in the ancient temple or tabernacle. Many kinds of sacrifices were offered, and as society became more complex the types of sacrifices multiplied; but for all of them an altar was necessary. Men believed at first that when they offered a sacrifice it was consumed by the Deity, either actually or in vaporized form. Originally, men ate the meal with the God; later the meal was placed on the altar for the God.

There were a number of special requirements for the construction of the altar. First, it had to be light enough for transportation from place to place, so it was a light frame covered with necessary metal. The altar was seven and a half feet square and four and a half feet high, with a step, or ledge, upon which the priest could stand. In addition, at each corner of the altar there was a horn. The origin of the horn is lost to us, but it may be a modification of original animal horns. These animal horns were either from animals offered in sacrifice (see *ABC*, p. 779*b*) or on animal heads supporting the altar. In any case, we know that the horns had special significance. A man fleeing from his pursuers could run to the altar and place his hands upon the horns and then be safe from capture. It was the primitive way of protecting the fugitive from unjust and hasty action of his accusers. Judge and jury have since made such "sanctuary" unnecessary.

The tabernacle was divided into two parts, and neither was open to the people, who met in the great court surrounding the sanctuary. Here began the separation between priest and laity, with a growing emphasis upon the priest as mediator between man and God.

The light (vv. 20-21) seems at first to have burned only throughout the night. If this was the case, then its purpose was illumination; or perhaps it was a symbol of the pillar of fire from desert tradition. It was only later that the lamp came to signify the Eternal Presence and was kept burning permanently.

Reading 45: Exodus 28

The term "priest" has come to have an offensive sound to many deeply religious people because of association of the term with sacrifice and ecclesiasticism. That is unfortunate, for this attitude has prevented them from seeing the fine offices that may be performed by the conscientious priest. The priest was much more than the one who presided at the altar—he was a counselor, a teacher, a judge, often a doctor, and always the pastor. Contrast is usually made between priest and prophet. That too is unfortunate, for it is usually done to the credit of the prophet and the disparagement of the priest. Priest and prophet each had his place—and each an important one. The prophets in Israel were seldom teachers or pastors. They were revolutionists, but their high ideals became a challenge to the priests who sought to lead their people to constantly higher levels of living. Without the priests the religion of Israel would have ceased to be, for they conserved the values and traditions of the past, and they interpreted the challenges of the prophets in the light of the new religious experiences of Israel.

Special clothing was to be used by the priest in his ministrations. The purpose of the sacred vestments was not so much to impress the people as to remind the priest of his office and his responsibility to God and man. Could any man read the engraving "Sacred to the Lord" (vv. 36-38) without being challenged? The decoration of the oracle pouch (vv. 15f.) was for the specific purpose of reminding the priest that he was a servant of the entire people.

The stones Urim and Thummin (v. 30) were used in the oracle pouch (vv. 15f.). They were probably the same size, shape, and weight but of different color. One stone meant "yes," the other "no." When the priest appeared before the altar seeking an answer to a problem, he stated it so that it could be answered simply. After appropriate ritual he put his hand into the pouch and drew out one stone, the answer to his problem. Many similar techniques are known to have been practiced in that day.

The tinkling of the bell was for the protection of the priest and was a warning to the Deity that the priest was about to enter his presence. Contrast the use of the bell in the mass of the Roman Catholic Church.

Every part of the priest's vestments was designed to remind him of his duty as a priest to the people and of his humanity in the presence of the divine.

Written Work.—Write a 500-word statement on the subject "The Values and Dangers of Symbolism in Religion." What are some symbols or forms which we use today? Of what help are they in worship? What dangers go with their use? This assignment may be prepared either as a simple statement or as an outline for a sermon on this topic.

Reading 46: Exodus 30:1-38

We may note briefly some of the further provisions for the priesthood and the sanctuary. An incense altar was designed to be placed in front of the veil of the Holiest Place. This seems to have been a provision from after the time of Solomon, and in ch. 27 the altar to stand before the veil seems to have been the one for burnt offerings. There was definite need for incense in those days. The slaughtering of animals and the burning of them must have created a problem in odors. The original use of incense was indeed to make the smell pleasant to God—and man.

The use of the sacred shekel as an offering was a distinctly late practice of Judaism. Coinage was not known until the seventh century B.C., nor the use of sacred money in Palestine until much later. This reference is but one of the many indications that this section of Exodus is part of the latest writings in the Books of the Law.

Cleanliness of the priesthood was provided for in part by the bronze laver. Shortage of water in Palestine almost guaranteed that the priests would arrive at the place of worship unbathed. (Provision is made here for the washing of hands and feet, for they were the most exposed parts of the body in travel.) Cleanliness of the priesthood was a common demand in the ancient East. In ancient Egypt the priest was required to shave from head to foot to guarantee freedom from vermin and dirt.

Sacred anointing oil and incense served the same purpose. There was an additional purpose for oil. Anything touched with it was sacred, and therefore taboo. Somewhat illogically, anyone coming in contact with an object so anointed became unclean. The provision that no layman could use the oil, and that neither priest nor layman could use incense (or perfume) just to smell good, was sound. This was not a provision against perfumes, certainly not against cosmetics, as some have insisted; it was simply a matter of

81

association. The East has long known the value of perfume. When men smelled this particular incense, by association their minds were turned to the sanctuary and all that it stood for.

Reading 47: Exodus 32:1-35

This is another dramatic story. It starts with the long absence of Moses. The people, tired of waiting for him, now seek to return to something familiar. The religion of Moses was apparently new to many of the Hebrews. They request that Aaron will make for them "a god." A mold is found. The metal from jewelry is used and a casting made. Two questions arise. Where did the mold come from? Why did the mold have the shape of a bull? The answer is the same in each case: Egyptian influence. The bull god Apis was well known in Egypt, and in all likelihood to the Hebrews. The mold also was undoubtedly of Egyptian origin. The people were simply reverting to something familiar. Aaron's excuse to Moses is an example of weakness in reasoning seldom paralleled: "And out came this bull" (v. 24b—American Trans.). Years later, when Jeroboam was bidding for a popular following, he set up gold calves, or bulls, and as he presented them to the people at Dan and Bethel, he said: "Behold your gods, O Israel, who brought you up from the land of Egypt" (1 Kings 12:28b—American Trans.). He, too, appealed to familiar patterns.

The remainder of the chapter is a gruesome story of murder in the name of religion. The conduct of Moses and the Levites must be judged in the light of the moral standards of that day, not ours. There was division in the camp, and for the safety of the loyal followers of Jehovah it was necessary to take violent action. The story was used later in defense of the Levitical priesthood. In the confession of Moses to God, and in his statement to the people, there is no condemnation of the slaughter; the sin confessed is that of bull worship. Relationship to God was through the group, not on an individual basis. It was not until the teaching of Jeremiah that men came to

82

understand that religion is necessarily an individual matter. In Moses' day the community had to be kept pure by purging from it those who sinned. The punishment of God would come upon the entire group, they believed. The community, therefore, took action before Moses prayed to God. The action may have been drastic, but it was sincere and according to accepted standards. Dare we pray for forgiveness until we have done what we can to make atonement? Forgiveness is an important part of religion. One of man's greatest needs is the knowledge that he can be forgiven. Confession must precede forgiveness. Is there need also to make amends for our sins? Certainly, if we have hurt others by our acts we should do what we can to repair that damage. When a man comes to his pastor and makes confession sincerely—perhaps the most humiliating experience he undergoes—dare that pastor say, "Oh, that's all right; just forget it"? One church leader has discovered that if he can help men to make amends, they feel that their prayer for forgiveness can be sincerely made. If they have hurt society or the church they accept tasks that will help to build the thing they have hurt. That is intelligent penitence. Contrast that standard with the action of the Levites.

Reading 48: Exodus 34:17-28

This is one of the earliest law codes known in Hebrew literature. It shows growth through many editings, yet at the beginning of each phrase can be seen the original form of the law. The third law (vv. 19-20) is a particularly good one to show development of thought. First there was a law which directed that all first-born life belonged to God and must be sacrificed, whether man or beast. The next step was to make possible the redemption of asses, which were economically very important. Finally, as religious insight developed, there was provision for the redemption of human life. Yet there are indications that human sacrifice was not unknown in later times (see 2 Kings 3:27; Lev. 27:28f.; Judges 11:31, 34; Mic. 6:7).

83

The entire list of laws is one that would apply only to agricultural life. These are religious observances that could be kept only by a farmer. It probably was the law code of the Canaanite before the Hebrews came into Palestine. All offerings to God must be set aside first, then men could use the rest. What would happen in our churches if our people would accept the standard of taking out God's share first, instead of giving to the church out of what they have left after all other obligations have been met? True trusteeship lies in meeting God's claim first, not in the particular percentage we give.

It is not enough to say that these laws regulated merely the mechanical aspects of religion. Such observances were extremely important in that day. Men had not yet come to see how religion was concerned with human welfare and the relation of man to man. Man had to begin by saying, "Is my conduct right in the sight of God?" Sacrifices were the great acts of religion, therefore it was important that these sacrifices should be carefully, regularly, and properly made. A sacrifice properly offered would please God, and would result in God's making a generous response to man's plea. But if God were angered by man's careless conduct at sacrifice, or an inferior offering, then the result for man would be terrible. We are grateful that man has been liberated from such beliefs. Religious pioneers dared to raise questions, and the time came when a prophet like Hosea could declare that God desired "mercy and not sacrifice" (Hos. 6:6).

Reading 49: Exodus 35:1-19; 36:2-7

In connection with these selections read *ABC*, p. 277*b*. As noted in *ABC*, much of the material in chs. 35-40 is simply repetition of earlier parts of the book of Exodus. This section may have been a separate handbook for the priests, since it is so full of details of the construction and the services of the sanctuary. The early part of ch. 35 tells of the kinds of contributions made by the people. Not only were there gifts of metals and materials, but those who

84

had skills and those who had confidence in their abilities came offering their services. The generosity of the people is portrayed in the opening verses of the next chapter. Perhaps this is only a priest's dream, but it has been discovered repeatedly that when people are persuaded of the worthiness of a project, little is needed to stir their enthusiasm, and their response is great. One great metropolitan newspaper publishes each year, some time before Christmas, a list of children whose Christmas is likely to be an unhappy one. It makes no appeal for them, but the response is tremendous. Each year hundreds of children are cared for in this way. The secret of the response to Moses' appeal seems to be that people could see directly the result of their work or gift. There was the fabric that they had made, or there was the metal that had been skillfully worked by their neighbor. A modern failure in church, and other fields, has been the great distance between the giver and the final use of the gift. Are we tapping resources in our own communities and churches? Not necessarily for money. We have assumed that only people with certain gifts could be of service to the church. Can you teach? Are you a good bookkeeper, or treasurer? But here is a stenographer. How she could aid her harried pastor whose correspondence is falling behind! Another can operate the mimeograph more skillfully than he, but can she be led to see that her work can be of significance in the church? One of the secrets of church administration is finding and harnessing many kinds of help. Even more important is the fact that we shall be serving people better when we find for them challenging tasks for which they are specially trained. Their happiness in their new responsibility will gladden the heart of any pastor.

Similarly, we must vitalize our appeal for mission work by making it very personal. Let us know the workers and the people with whom they work. We are working to save people, not to raise a given number of dollars. The tabernacle being built by Moses and his followers was a long-needed building, but, more than that, it was their own.

They had personal pride, joy, and *participation* in its construction. That is why they responded so well.

Written Work.—Make a list of the ways in which people could serve your church. Which of these tasks are now being performed by the pastor? Which could be delegated to some other person? State briefly how you would make an appeal to your church for help in these activities. Indicate how your church could be of more service to its community if you could find new kinds of leadership.

VI

THE POWER OF THE PRIESTHOOD
Leviticus

THE book of Leviticus is the sixth section of the Books of the Law. Its name is difficult to pronounce, its meaning is not well understood, and the contents of the book seem far from our interests today and of little consequence in our present-day problems. Careful reading, however, leads one to discover in this book gems of religious experience. One is constantly reminded in reading Leviticus that the heart of religious problems is the same in every age. The essence of religion is man's right relation to God. Salvation is the means by which that relationship is established. Man can be religious without coming into satisfactory relationship with his fellow man, though we may question whether he can be Christian. But man cannot be religious and leave God out of consideration. In the later years of Hebrew history, salvation was thought to be a constant process obtained by the offering of proper sacrifices through the priest. Only a priest could plead with God for man. Protestants have insisted upon "the priesthood of all believers," but we must confess that many Protestants have forgotten this or have failed to assume the priestly office. Likewise, we have erred in assuming that an experience of conversion is the only thing needful for salvation. It is imperative that man shall know the love of God, obtain forgiveness for sin, and pledge his allegiance to God through Christ. He then begins a new way of living, seeking to meet the challenge of the high standard of the Christ way of life. This is a constant process, daily lived. Men have discovered that there are certain religious practices which, if observed day by day, will strengthen a man in his religious purposes. Prayer, reading the Bible, praise, and meditation are some of the means by which we can minister to our daily religious needs. To minister in this way is to practice the priestly office in the Protestant sense. And if we minister as priests for our families in their needs, then we have become a "royal priesthood," worthy to be known as followers of Christ.

The book of Leviticus deals with six problems of ritualistic religion. The first seven chapters give directions for the proper offerings of various sacrifices. Chs. 8-10 list the regulations for the consecration of priests, beginning with the rites performed for Aaron. The next five chapters give regulations for deciding when men and animals are clean enough, or holy enough, to participate in the ritual. Ch. 16 describes the Day of Atonement. Chs. 17-25 are a unit coming from an early day, and are known as the "Holiness Code." This code of law gives regulations for preserving holy cleanliness in the community at all times. The final chapters (26-27) list promises, warnings, and laws concerning vows.

If we recognize that Leviticus is concerned primarily with salvation and with the daily religious needs of those who believed that salvation is a continuous process, then we shall discover the rich message of the book. To be sure, there is much that is uninteresting and unimportant for the modern reader, but it will be our purpose to discover the passages of richest value.

Reading 50: Leviticus 1

Every sinful act results in a hurt either to ourselves or to those about us. The harm done varies greatly. The religion of Israel demanded different sacrifices for different types of guilt. Five types of offerings are named in the early chapters of Leviticus: burnt-offering, meal-offering, peace-offering or thank-offering, sin-offering, and guilt-offering. It is not clear how some of these sacrifices originated. There was no attempt to work out a system of graded penalties. Custom just "grew up," and sometimes there is confusion concerning the differences between the various types of offerings. Religious practices are not always logical developments. The worshiper may be conscious of good that he believes is the result of his prayer or sacrifice. He then seeks to remember the exact wording or the precise ritual he used, believing that he has discovered the right religious technique. Constant repetition leads to a fixed pattern, or "ritual." Does God demand that we shall always worship with the same order of service? Write in your notebook the *dangers* of formalities in religion. What are the *advantages* for us as ministers in the thorough preparation of the order of worship, of our prayers as well as of our sermons?

The burnt-offering was a gift to God, and it was to be entirely consumed by fire. Only domesticated male animals or birds could be sacrificed in this way. It was a farmer's, not the hunter's, gift to God. A male animal was an expensive gift to make, and it is possible that men were tempted to give an animal that was useless to them because of some imperfection. Provision was therefore made that only a perfect animal could be offered. This was sound religious thinking. The emphasis was upon the cost to the giver and not the possible result to the Deity. Another provision of similar significance was based upon ability to pay. A wealthy man gave an ox, the poor man a bird. The justice of these provisions was upset by traders in Jesus' day, and it was this that aroused his anger (see Mk. 11:15f.).

The final test to be applied to the offering was: "Will this please God?" Can we apply this test to our offerings today? We serve God and his church by deeds. We support the church by our offerings. Can we test each act and each gift by asking, "Will this please God?" What pleases God, the gift or the attitude of the giver? The Hebrews did not "take a collection"; the people made an offering that was a sacrifice. Are our standards of giving on a higher level or a lower level of religious thinking?

89

Reading 51: Leviticus 3

The Hebrew word *shelem* is usually translated "peace-offering" but sometimes is rendered "thank-offering" (see *ABC*, p. 280). Neither gives a satisfactory meaning for this Hebrew sacrifice. It apparently was offered in a spirit of thankfulness for the purpose of maintaining harmony and peace between the worshiper and the Deity. It was the ancient method of keeping the spiritual accounts in balance, or possibly of putting the worshiper on the credit side of the ledger. We shall disagree with the theology, and we shall insist that man can never repay the benefits he has received from God; but perhaps we can sympathize with the ancient who wanted to do more than just meet his obligations.

With all animal offerings there was strict provision that the caul of the liver was to be consumed by fire. The livers of sacrificed animals in ancient Babylon were used to divine the fates. Hundreds of tablets have been recovered from Babylonia that give us complete information about how to read the markings of the liver for divining purposes. It is possible that the provision to burn the caul of the liver was merely an attempt to prevent Babylonian magical practices in Palestine.

Breast fat and blood were also forbidden to human consumption. We have no clear explanation concerning the prohibition of breast fat for food. One suggestion is that it was considered a special delicacy and therefore particularly desirable as an offering. In the case of the blood, we are better informed. It was considered to be the essence of life and therefore to belong to the Creator. One of the strict requirements of kosher meat for Jews today is that the blood shall have been drained from the animal. To insure this, the beast is killed by the prescribed method of the ancient Jews. Its throat is slit by the rabbi, and the carcass is hung so as to let all blood drain from it. Lifeblood must not be consumed. There are more references to the blood of sacrifice in Leviticus than in any other book in the Bible.

When the necessary restrictions had been observed, the remainder of the animal could be consumed by the donor. The priest was entitled to a share in return for his services (see Lev. 7:31-34, and below, *Reading* 82).

Reading 52: Leviticus 4:1-35; 5:5-13

When the emphasis of religion is upon the observance of rites and ceremonies, then the worshiper must be very careful that all religious acts are correctly performed, and it is always possible to make a mistake or forget some observance. It then becomes necessary to make provision for the correction of such mistakes. The sin-offering of ancient Israel served this purpose. It was to cleanse the individual from uncleanness which had come to him by reason of contact with unclean things, things that were taboo, or from some thoughtless act which violated religious restriction. The penalty to be paid varied according to the importance of the individual in the community, the priest being at the top of the list and the citizen without leadership responsibility at the bottom. This provision reflects the importance of the priesthood in the postexilic period, and indicates also the less important place of political leadership.

The weakness of ceremonial religion is clearly evidenced in this chapter. It was this very weakness that prevented the priest and the Levite from ministering to the man who fell among thieves. If they had touched the man and he was already dead, then they would have become unclean and could not have proceeded to Jerusalem to perform the religious ceremonials. Jesus taught by this parable "Your religious observances get in the way of true religious conduct" (see Lk. 10:25-37). Jesus not only answered the question concerning one's neighbor but he also gave us a test of religious living. There are two dangers always present in religious ceremonial. First, there is danger of substituting the observance of the form for religious living. Second, there is danger of confusing the thrill that may come from beauty and orderliness with vital religious experience

91

Beauty, order, and dignity are needed in our services of worship, but let us make certain that they lead us to communion with God and do not become substitutes for that communion.

No provision is made for sacrifice as a penalty for intentional wrong. Sin-offerings were made for unintentional acts of wrong conduct. Sin is sometimes defined as an act willfully committed in defiance or neglect of divine Law. Such conduct in ancient Israel would have resulted in the individual's being driven from the community, for the Hebrews believed that only in this way could the community be protected. They believed also that there was no hope for an individual who willfully violated religious laws. The Hebrews considered that they were bound together by religious ties and were a congregation rather than a political body. Therefore an individual who violated or would not accept the religious standards was necessarily excluded from the group. The action was parallel to that of a modern church which expels from membership those found guilty of unchristian conduct. List in your notebook the arguments for and against such group action.

Reading 53: Leviticus 8:1-35; 6:20-23

One's first reaction on reading this assignment is that it contains too much of pomp and ceremony that is meaningless. But let us not be too hasty in judgment. The priest was an absolute necessity in the religion of that day, and to be installed as priest was to be placed in a position of great significance. The importance of the position justified the elaborate ceremony of induction into office. Danger came when priests accepted all of the privileges and assumed few of the responsibilities of their office. It was this that led to the condemnation of the priesthood. For that man who was ready and willing to undertake the duties of priesthood, the installation service was quite meaningful.

The installation lasted for seven days, the ceremony consisting of bathing, being clothed with priestly garments, consecration with oil, and the offering of special sacrifices on behalf of the priests. On the eighth day the new priests were ready to perform sacrifices in their own right. We know little about the formal and practical preparation of candidates for the priesthood. We shall confess, too, that an impressive ordination service would not make a good priest unless he was properly trained. Nevertheless, the young candidate must have looked forward with anticipation, and perhaps dread, to the week's program of ordination. Happy is that minister who can look back with satisfaction upon his own admission to the office of deacon or elder. It is important for the candidate for any high office that he shall not be permitted to enter it without proper appreciation of the new responsibility that he must assume. A dignified and meaningful service is important if for no other reason than that it may be a means of inspiring the candidate to be his best self. Certainly the vow made as a man undertakes priestly or pastoral office in the church should be one of the most significant acts of his life and should, like a costly jewel, be mounted in the finest setting.

The Hebrews knew the importance that ceremonial had also for the people. In this case they perhaps could not witness any of it except the first time the new priests offered sacrifices. But the separation of the young men from the community for seven days, with their appearance at the end, now dressed in their new robes of office, undoubtedly had its effect. The Hebrews learned that unless the church itself surrounded its leadership with dignity, laymen could not be expected to have as much confidence. What dangers or what advantages are there in elaborate ceremonial? Put your answers in your notebook.

Reading 54: Leviticus 11

Judaism has continued to lay great stress upon abstinence from unclean food and the ability to distinguish clean, or kosher, food. It is probable that the early protest against the pig came as reaction to the religious practices of people with whom the Hebrews came in contact, there being some evidence that swine played an important part in religious sacrifice of early inhabitants of Palestine. We do know that it was difficult for the Hebrews to work out relatively simple tests of cleanliness, for they had through the years designated a number of animals and birds that did not fit a single classification. With animals and seafood it was made fairly simple, but insects, birds, and reptiles had to be named individually. We probably shall never know why some were classified as unclean, but in a few cases we do have information. The snake, or serpent, was unclean. It is identified with evil throughout Hebrew Scriptures. The Canaanites, on the other hand, thought highly of the snake, and it appears constantly in the religious symbolism of the Baal religion.

Jesus protested against the blind and inhuman legalism that came as a result of regulations of this type. He stated that it is not what enters a man's mouth that makes him clean or unclean but the things that come out of his mouth (Mk. 7:15-23). It is on this basis that Christianity has said that we are liberated from the old legalism of the Jews.

The vision of Peter also comes to our minds in this connection. Peter's vision was based on this restriction of the Jew (see Acts 10:9-15). Then came the conviction: "Do not call what God has cleansed unclean" (Acts 10:15—*American Trans.*). What is the test of whether or not food is good for human consumption? We are reminded, however, of Paul's statement that he would not eat meat (that had been sacrificed to idols) because of his companion's religious convictions (see 1 Cor. 8:4-13). The Salvation Army does not observe the sacrament of the Lord's Supper because the use of wine or grape juice in a religious service in which many of the people have been rescued from slavery in liquor might result in their relapse to former habits. The Hebrews recognized that everyday patterns of thought and religion often have influence upon each other, and many of the Hebrew laws are safeguards against wrong thinking. Sometimes it happened that men forgot the reason for the law and its observance became merely mechanical.

Finally, we need to raise a question here regarding those sincere people who affirm that they believe the Bible from "cover to cover." Yet they eat pork, oysters, and other things specifically prohibited. What do we mean by "belief"? Surely it ought to mean something by which we can live. The literal accuracy of the account may be unimportant for religious living, and interesting only for historical record. Our Scripture is important, not because it records events and customs of an ancient people, but because it preserves great religious principles upon which man can build his life.

Reading 55: Leviticus 12

This short chapter is an expression of an attitude toward childbirth that is unfortunate. Today we talk of the beauties of motherhood, and we believe the relationship between mother and child to be one of the finest expressions of love in the world. Yet the Hebrews asserted that when a woman gave birth to a child she was ceremonially unclean, and needed to be purified before she could again be an acceptable member of society. Why? Their attitude arose partly from ignorance and partly from superstition. Women and children were relatively unimportant members of that ancient society. The act of childbirth was surrounded by mystery, and it was thought that good and evil forces surrounded the mother. Then, too, the Hebrew seems to have followed the simple rule that any discharge of the body makes the person unclean. After childbirth there is a discharge that lasts approximately forty days. Therefore the mother was pronounced unclean for that length of time. Why that time was doubled in the case of giving birth to a girl is not clear.

Luke is fully aware of Jewish custom based upon this chapter. He tells of the circumcision of Jesus after eight days (Lk. 2:21), and of the later presentation in the Temple after the (forty-day) period of the purification of

Mary (2:22-23). He knows also of the provision that the poor could sacrifice turtledoves instead of an animal (2:24).

Mating and parenthood are expressions of the finest relationships known to man and should be portrayed as such instead of associating both with shame, as is so frequently done. In ancient Israel continence for forty days, which was enjoined by law, had its origin in superstition. The modern physician recommends it for the safety and comfort of the mother. We are grateful that superstition gave some protection to the young mother, and we must insist that that protection shall still be given—but insist also that the mother is neither unclean nor a person of shame. Here is a case where a knowledge of the history of religion can free us from foolish fears and superstition.

Reading 56: Leviticus 13:1-17, 29-37, 45-46

The priest had many functions besides that of conducting the religious ceremonials. These chapters indicate his responsibility as a medical examiner for the community. Formal learning of all kinds was one of the responsibilities of the church, and there were no doctors, lawyers, nor teachers apart from the priesthood. The guidance and protection of the community were definite responsibilities of the church. Read the article in a good encyclopedia on "history of medicine" to discover the part that religion has played in the development of medical knowledge. When were medical studies separated from the church? What were the gains or losses to the medical profession resulting from this separation? Put your discoveries in your notebook.

Read *ABC*, pp. 287-88. The term "leprosy" was used to designate any skin infection in which there was an eruption. People knew nothing of germs in those days, but they were aware of contagion. Leprous individuals were separated from the community, and their life was not a happy one. Living outside of the village or city walls, alone, they were required to cry "Unclean, unclean" whenever other people approached. The problem of getting food was a real one, and they were usually limited to the food that a few charitable people left for them outside the city walls. Nothing was done to cure the disease or alleviate their pain and suffering. The great problem was to protect the community. Isolation hospitals are possible today only because our medical doctors have learned how to protect those who must serve the sick in those hospitals. The problem in medicine has been to protect the larger body of society and then to give aid to the individual. In nearly every disease we have learned how to do both. Where we can help the individual only at the risk of exposing society, are we justified in helping that individual? Fortunately that problem does not confront us in contagious diseases today. But what of the problems of delinquency and crime? Which must we think of first, the individual or society?

Modern research has led to our discovery that true leprosy is one of the least contagious among the communicable diseases. Equally important is our modern knowledge that disease comes from germs and is often due to the conditions under which men are forced to live. The ancients believed that all sickness came as the result of sin, either of the individual or of his parents. Men are now learning that it is possible for society to sin against the individual, but that often it is the individual who suffers. If you know a physician or police officer in a large city, ask him to show you a "spot map" of delinquency or of tuberculosis. Note that in the crowded and low-rent areas there is more disease and crime. Note how few spots there are in those areas where wealthly people live. What is your friend's explanation of these conditions? Does the chuch still have a responsibility in this problem?

Written Work.—Write an essay on "The Priesthood," showing the requirements necessary to enter the priesthood, the ceremonies of installation, and the duties of the priesthood listed in the chapters you have read in Leviticus.

Reading 57: Leviticus 16

The Day of Atonement is one of the most important days in the Jewish calendar. It comes on the tenth day of the new year. The Jewish year begins (in September or October) with ten days of penitence, and the tenth day is Yom Kippur, the Day of Atonement, when each congregation in Israel fasts and prays and seeks spiritual revival. The origin of this day of confession is unknown, but indications are that in early times these acts of atonement could be performed whenever it was thought necessary for the good and safety of the community. Later, as indicated by vv. 29-34, the observance of this rite was restricted to once a year. V. 29 names the tenth day of the seventh month of the new religious year, which had been introduced from Babylon, but on the other calendar it was at the beginning of the year.

The sacrifices included a ram for a burnt-offering, a bullock for a sin-offering, and in addition two he-goats. One of these goats was sacrificed upon the altar as a sin-offering, and the other was led to the desert bearing the sins of the community. Not only was the community to be purged of uncleanness, but the altar and sanctuary also required atonement in their behalf (read *ABC,* pp. 169f.) .

There were good and bad results from the observance of this custom. It was good for the community and for the individual to face themselves periodically and to feel that they were accountable to God for their conduct. My Roman Catholic friends tell me that it is a fearful thing to attend the confessional. It has sometimes been charged that the system of the confessional is mechanical, with sins glibly confessed and penances just as easily discharged. This is not true where confession is sincere before God and the sinner seeks to make atonement. But the danger in the confessional was the danger in the Hebrew Day of Atonement, that of being a mechanical discharge of religious duties. It was this that led Jesus to insist (Mt. 5:23f.) that one's gift should not be presented at the altar until one had made right the wrongs he had done to a brother. The greatest danger in making confession, whenever or wherever we may make it, is that we shall not be completely honest with ourselves or with God. We seek to excuse ourselves instead of admitting that we were wrong. Often we seek to shift the blame to others. The man who confesses a fault and is genuinely sorry will not as easily commit that same fault as the individual whose confession is insincere or deceitful. One of the big problems of any religious leader is to get men to look at themselves sincerely. The Day of Atonement was one means of doing this among the Hebrews.

Reading 58: Leviticus 18

This chapter is concerned with the cleanliness of the marriage relation. The Hebrew had no special word for marriage, and he expressed it by saying to "take a woman," "to love a woman," "to know a woman," or to "uncover her nakedness." The warnings in vv. 2-5 against the practices of the Egyptians and Canaanites had political and religious significance. It was the custom in both countries, especially among the ruling classes, to marry within the family. In Egypt, at least, we have evidence that this was done to keep power and wealth within certain families. In the Baal religion the god of fertility always married his sister, and there may have been religious protest by the Hebrews in these laws of marriage.

We know, too, that the nature religion of Baal put unnecessary emphasis upon cohabitation, and it insisted that ritual cohabitation at religious festivals was necessary for the fructification of the earth. One of the hardest battles that the prophets and priests had to fight was that of keeping the religion of Israel from going in the same direction. Laws were enacted in Israel to guard zealously the marriage relationship and to direct the thinking of Israel away from the low sex desires. Excavations of the archaeologist and passages such as Jer. 44:19 and Hos. 4:13-14 indicate that these laws were not obeyed by many of the people.

99

All communities have recognized eventually that regulation of marriage is necessary. The church has accepted this list (vv. 6-18), now known as "degrees of marriage," and it is generally observed in modern society. Modern medical science has given us the reasons against the inbreeding of families. The Hebrews had made their discovery through observation.

In the marriage ceremony we state that "the family is the foundation of human fellowship." Does this mean that those performing the ceremony have a part in laying the structure of society? What responsibility does the minister have to society when he unites two persons in marriage? He is an officer of the state, and in many states he must be licensed by the state. Does that mean that his responsibility ceases when he sees that the requirements of the state have been complied with? He is also a minister of the church, and the church usually has higher standards than the state. What are the minister's responsibilities as a representative of the church? Can we excuse low standards by saying, "If I do not marry them some other preacher will?" The Hebrews placed at the beginning of the Holiness Code their concern for purity in marriage. They knew that unless purity was guarded here they could not expect holiness in society.

Reading 59: Leviticus 19:1-18

The Holiness Code held an extremely high standard for men in their dealings with God and man. Vv. 2-4 summarize the Ten Commandments, and vv. 5-8 summarize the laws of sacrifice. Concern for the poor or resident alien appears in vv. 9-10. The low economic standard of living is indicated in v. 13; it was forbidden to hold a man's wages overnight, for he needed his money and it was wrong to withhold it. This same standard is in the background of Jesus' parable in Mt. 20:1-16, where the laborers are paid off at the end of the day's work.

It would be difficult to find a higher standard of conduct than that of v. 14. In effect it states: "Take no action against

100

any individual who cannot be aware of your action or who is not in a position to defend himself." Does this prohibit cursing a man in language he does not understand, or the individual who is not within hearing distance? Is the man who sets a trap for an unwary fellow employee, for his own gain, guilty of violating the principle of this law?

Can you think of members of your own church who may be guilty of the sin of talebearing condemned in v. 16? What can a pastor do to prevent members of his congregation from coming to him with stories about his predecessor? How many pastors secure their own professional life by telling derogatory stories about fellow pastors? Is this not forbidden in this same verse?

To love one's own countrymen does not mean freedom to hate one's enemies (see Mt. 5:43). But how many of us have arrived at the place of loving the people of our own land, of whatsoever color or economic level? Are we consistent in our religious conduct in giving to missions and then refusing to sit with a Negro, a Mexican, or an American of Japanese ancestry?

The standard in this chapter and throughout the Holiness Code is "This must be your conduct, because I am your God." The close relationship between God and man is in the background of the code. Here was man's part of the Covenant.

Reading 60: Leviticus 24:10-23

There is almost no narrative in the book of Leviticus, but here a brief story is introduced to give the setting for the Law of Retaliation. Desert and tribal law had demanded blood for blood, but it usually happened that when intertribal warfare broke out there was no limit. Murder by another tribesman usually was the signal for revenge by the murdered man's fellow tribesmen, and they took as many lives in exchange as they could get. The Law of Retaliation restricted all this; the point of emphasis in this section is not "take your revenge" but rather "take only one life for a life, one eye for one eye," and so on. This law should

101

therefore be named the Law of Justice, and not the Law of Retaliation. As noted in *ABC*, p. 295, this standard is far below the Christian standard of forgiveness, but it was a step beyond the old idea of vengeance and brought men to the place of justice. It meant in the case of murder that the culprit should be apprehended and pay the death penalty. Where only one life could be taken, society would make certain that the life paid was that of the guilty party whenever possible.

Death was the penalty for blasphemy, whether by a regular member of the religious community or by one adopted into the community. This is another demonstration that the community was considered primarily a religious unit rather than a political group. Because the Jew had great fear that he might use the name of God wrongly, there developed the custom of referring to the Deity by titles instead of the personal name. For this reason we do not know how the personal name of God was pronounced by the Hebrews. The name Jehovah may have been pronounced originally "Yahweh"; we have just the four letters *YHWH* or *JHVH* without any vowels in our MSS. Another reason the Hebrews refused to pronounce the personal name of God was in order that Gentiles could not use the name of God for curses, a practice common in Persian and Greek times. It is still considered good religion to respect the name of God.

Reading 61: Leviticus 25:1-17, 25-28, 35-38

Much of the Holiness Code is devoted to instruction concerning sacrifice, the priesthood, and the sacred festivals; but occasionally there are provisions which more intimately concern the layman. These regulations are regularly on a high moral plane. The cultural and economic standards, however, differ greatly from those of modern times. This assignment includes laws which deal with the Sabbath of the land, the basis of land prices, and interest charges.

The land must rest, just as man rested. People knew nothing in that day about rotation of crops, fertilization, or other modern scientific methods of crop production; but they had discovered that the yield of the ground was greater if it was allowed to rest for one season. Likewise, the seventh seventh year was to be followed by a year of rest and jubilee. It is doubtful if these provisions were carried out to any great extent. As a matter of fact, the laws of the Sabbath of the land and the Jubilee of the land seem to have come from different periods, and probably both were not observed in the same period. If both laws were literally followed, then the land would be uncultivated in the forty-ninth and the fiftieth years. Poor peasants could not afford anything like that.

The sale price of the land depended upon the number of years from Jubilee. Land value varied with the number of crops that could be gathered before the next Jubilee. We may disagree with the economics, but the principle of the law was that the seller should give value for money. It was completely the reverse of the principle "let the buyer beware."

Liberty was to be granted in the Jubilee year to all inhabitants. If a man sold himself into serfdom he was entitled to his freedom after a period of service. The return of land and the freeing of serfs was apparently an attempt to prevent from happening in Palestine what had happened in other countries—namely, a few individuals' gaining control of property and people. This section of the Holiness Code is concerned with the rights and freedom of individuals. The Hebrews had discovered under the old system that if a man sold himself into slavery he rarely was freed. Interest rates and land values prevented him from redeeming himself. In vv. 25f. it was provided that a poor man's kinsfolk should redeem him. It was provided further, in vv. 35-38, that interest could not be charged on money loaned to one's countrymen. Some people have tried to distinguish between "interest" and "usury," but this law provides that no interest shall be taken. All interest rates in that day were usurious. The principle here was simply to see that those in more fortunate circumstances should not

103

profit from another's misfortunes. We may raise a question here regarding those local churches which lend money on interest to less fortunate churches.

On what great symbol of American freedom is a portion of v. 10 inscribed? Is freedom possible unless we accept the basic principle upon which this verse is based, namely, concern for one's fellow man even though it may mean giving up personal gain of money or property?

Written Work.—Write "Ten Rules for Religious Living," basing your rules upon the principles found in Leviticus, but changing those principles where you believe that Christ's teachings demand it.

VII

OTHER STORIES OF DESERT WANDERINGS
Numbers

IN the book of Exodus, Moses is a towering figure; in Leviticus he recedes to the background; but in Numbers, Moses returns as the central personality and gives to the book its only semblance of unity. We know the book under the title "Numbers" from the numbering, or census, in the opening chapters. The Jews know it as "In the Wilderness," a more exact description. See *ABC*, p. 298. Numbers deals with the fortunes and misfortunes of Israel interwoven with laws and traditions of the nation. Its threefold division is noted in *ABC*, p. 298*b*.

It is apparent throughout that the collection was made from many different sources, one of which is named "The Book of the Wars of the Lord" (Num. 21:14). A number of fine poems, or at least fragments, have been preserved: "The Priestly Benediction" (6:24-26); "The Song of the Ark" (10:35-36); "The Song of the Boundary" (21:14-15); "The Song of the Well" (21:17-18); "A Song of Heshbon" (21:27-30); and "The Oracles of Balaam" (chs. 23-24), which contain four longer and three shorter poems concerning Israel and her enemies.

There is in Numbers much repetition from Exodus, Leviticus, and Deuteronomy; and in some cases there is difficulty in reconciling the narrative of this book with the order of events given in the other books of the Pentateuch. The Rev. Hugh Martin has aptly summarized the significance of this book for us (*The Story of the Bible*, I, 1716): "Numbers is a medley; vivid and thrilling narrative is in-

105

terspersed by dry legislative detail. But there is at least one unifying factor: amid much that can hardly fail to be tedious to the modern reader, much that is perplexing, and not a few passages that reflect sub-Christian views of God, there stands out vividly the figure of Moses. The stories of his selfless devotion to his people's welfare, his courage and his undaunted faith in the face of rebellion and opposition, combine to present to the imagination a majestic and heroic personality."

We should note also that the book is quite frank in its portrayal of the Hebrews, who did not always recognize the greatness of their leader and often complained about Moses' leadership, sometimes going to the extreme of accusing him of bad faith and selfish motives.

Reading 62: Numbers 5:1-10

The greatest responsibility which rested upon Moses was that of leading the people safely on their journey. It was therefore natural that laws should be formulated which placed the community and its interests ahead of the individual. But we should remember that the community was a group of individuals, and that the law simply sought to protect the larger number against those individuals whose selfish or thoughtless acts might bring bad results to the entire group. We know, of course, that the individual was not fully recognized until much later in history. Two groups of culprits are dealt with in these verses.

First, the unclean men and women were to be driven from the camp. There were three kinds of unclean people: those who were unclean by reason of leprosy, those who had any form of bodily discharge, and those who came into contact with a corpse. Re-entrance to the camp and community was by examination and permission of the priest. The regulation of expulsion seems harsh to us, but it was inevitable. There are times when organized society must say: "These are the standards by which you must live if you wish to remain in the group. If you violate these standards, then you must be removed, at least temporarily, from society." Today, instead of sending the family outside of the city when there is contagious disease, the medical officer nails a card on the house warning other people to stay away, and the members of the sick person's family must remain within their own house until freed by the proper authorities. The purpose is exactly the same as the provisions of this early Hebrew law, and changes in practice have come because of new medical knowledge.

Second, there was provision for the recompense to be made by those who had violated civil law. If a man had wrongfully come into possession of anything, he had to pay it back, if possible to the one from whom he took it or to his next of kin, and if there were no heirs, then to the priest. In every case repayment had to be made together with 20 per cent penalty. Note, too, that sin against mankind was considered breaking faith with God. This was because the community was considered a religious unit and every member of it assumed responsibilities before God as a member of the community. The modern parallel would be that of a man who assumes new responsibilities when he becomes a member of the church. He is now one of a religious group and has special responsibilities toward the members of that group. Of course he knows, too, by Christian teachings, that when he becomes a Christian he assumes new attitudes and obligations toward all other men.

Vv. 9-10 declare that the priest became the personal possessor of the contributions given to him. This regulation does not agree with the provision in Ezek. 44:28 which provides that priests shall have no inheritance or property. This disagreement was one of the reasons for the long debate to determine whether or not the prophecy of Ezekiel should be admitted to the Bible.

Reading 63: Numbers 5:11-31

The test indicated in this chapter seems crude to modern men, yet we may note that there is a certain truth involved. Psychologists have developed "lie detectors" which are based upon the same principle, human reaction under fear.

Presumably the main effect of this particular test was that, under the burden of fear, the culprit would break down in confession. Every preacher knows the dryness of throat and tongue that can come on some fearsome occasions. This physiological fact was the basis during the Middle Ages for the lie test. A flame or hot poker was applied to the tongue, and if the victim was burned he was judged guilty. Unfortunately, too many people were afraid because of the test itself and not because of guilt, and many an innocent victim paid the death penalty. Though the fact was not recognized by ancients, actually they were dealing with a fundamental human factor. Wrongdoing brings with it a sense of guilt that is a burden.

We usually think of a minister of religion as one who aids individuals in their confession in order that they may achieve a sense of peace and restoration. In this case the priest aids the suspicious husband, and is placed in the position of forcing a confession from the guilty individual. The priest was a lawyer, a prosecuting attorney, and a judge, whenever necessity demanded. There are still some churches that believe that the judgment of the church takes precedence over the civil courts, and that Christian people ought not to resort to the civil courts with their problems. How far should the church go in aiding in domestic or other difficulties? The church should develop right understanding and attitudes such as will lead to right marriages, help by teaching and influence to create Christian homes, counsel where difficulties appear, set its face against all that undermines the family life. Should the minister appeal to fear in order to obtain confession? Is there a distinction between presenting the facts of the possible consequences of wrongdoing, and picturing the "torments of hell" in the hope that the culprit will "flee from the wrath to come"?

It is probable that in ancient Israel there were sympathetic priests who were able, despite the severity of this test, to lead accused but innocent wives through the ordeal to the satisfaction of suspicious husbands. If the minister remembers that human understanding and sympathy must

108

always be his major guides, he will have a principle that will never fail him. It will not be as easy, sometimes, to interpret the law on this basis, and he may be tempted to apply literally the provisions of the law. Law always must be made to serve humanity, not be its master.

Reading 64: Numbers 6:1-27

This is the only place where we have record of the Law of Nazirites. In the period of the Judges the vow seems to have been kept by some people throughout life (Samson, Samuel). At a later period the vows were taken for a limited period only, probably in payment for some great blessing that had been received or was expected from God. In N.T. times the observance of the vows was possible in other lands than Palestine, if the experience of Paul is any criterion (Acts 18:18f.). The Nazirite vow was threefold: to abstain from wine, liquor, grapejuice, and grapes; to keep the hair and beard uncut; and to stay away from corpses. Originally the abstinences were attempts to keep the individuals free from the "uncleanness" of other religions. Refusal to partake of the vine or its products was in protest against the religion of Canaan, Baalism. Staying clear of the deceased undoubtedly had its origin in a protest against the worship of the dead, a practice common in Eastern lands. The provision against cutting the hair and beard is not quite so clear, but two practices of other people may give us guidance. Egyptian priests were clean shaven over the entire body. We know, also, that a part of the ceremonial worship of the dead was to sacrifice the hair of one's head and beard. Either of these practices could be the background of the second of the Nazirite vows.

The Nazirites were looked upon as lay ministers, or attendants at the shrine. Special offerings and ceremonial were necessary when their period of service had been completed. What their special responsibilities in service were we do not know, but in the late period of Bible history they were regarded highly and were the only persons besides the high priest permitted to enter the Holiest Place.

Vv. 22-27 contain the priestly blessing that has become so well known in the Christian Church and that is sometimes erroneously named after certain organizations, thus giving the impression that it originated with them. The prayer belongs to all groups, to Jews and Christians alike. Here is a prayer that can be used with graciousness by the Christian minister in those groups where Jews are present. Those who insist upon the literal interpretation of the Scriptures will have difficulty with these verses, for v. 23 states specifically that the blessing is to be used with Israelites, and v. 27 indicates that when it is used on behalf of Israelites, God would bless them. Nothing is said about Gentiles. The spirit of the prayer would gather in all those who acknowledge themselves the sons of God. Note also that this prayer began as a priestly blessing upon the congregation. We use it now for the entire group to commit each other into the care of God, the leader voicing the first phrase, the people the second, the entire group the third.

Reading 65: Numbers 8:5-19, 24-26

The Levite was an important person in the life of Israel. Turn to p. 1431 of the index of *ABC* and look up the many references under the word "Levite." Make a notation in your notebook of the important position the Levite held in the religious life of Israel. What were his duties? Did his position change during the history of the Hebrews? The ideal proposed was that every first-born son should be dedicated to God as a priest. That was the custom in the early days of Israel, but it was soon changed by substituting all Levites for every first-born, and priests had to come from the families of the Levites. During the Exile, Ezekiel proposed that only those in the family of Zadok should be priests, and the others should fill less important Temple roles (Ezek. 44:10-16; 1 Kings 2:35; 4:4) After the Exile, priests were chosen from the descendants of Aaron, and Levites became the Temple servants.

The period of service was from the ages of twenty-five to fifty years, but after reaching the age of fifty a Levite had the privilege of voluntary service. (See Num. 4:3, where service begins at thirty.) The financial support for the Levites is outlined in Num. 18:20-32.

The induction of Levites into their office was elaborate, but not as long or as involved as the consecration to the priesthood. The installation had three steps: (1) The candidates were thoroughly cleansed in body and clothing. (2) They were presented as an offering to God, or dedicated. (3) Finally, they were made representative of the community by having the community leaders place their hands on the candidates' heads. It is possible that their being offered as a wave-offering has this same significance (v. 11). The offering of sin and burnt-offerings may be considered part of the acts of cleansing. The purposes of these three steps were: (1) to make sure that the candidates were acceptable to God; (2) to present the candidates to God and to have them accepted; and (3) to indicate that they represented all families in the community. We usually think of a candidate for church service as dedicating himself to that service, but ancient Israel dedicated the entire community through the candidate. Some denominations at the installation of a minister as pastor of a church give an opportunity for the congregation to commit themselves to the service of the church by asking them to promise to aid and work with the newly installed pastor.

Reading 66: Numbers 11:1-15

Too many are unwilling to pay the price of liberation. This was true of the people mentioned in this chapter. They longed for the good food they had known in Egypt. They were unwilling to suffer the consequences of crossing the desert to liberty. Many people have refused to be converted because of their unwillingness to give up some pleasure that was important to them. At least we admire their honesty in recognizing the need to make sacrifice.

We may be sympathetic with the angry outburst of Moses. He had suffered much as the leader, and anyone burdened with leadership can fully understand his sense of frustration. Let us not dismiss it easily by saying, "That is wicked." Jeremiah cursed the day of his birth, but he became the instrument of great religious progress. Only as he approached maturity did Jeremiah learn to control his outbursts. Even Jesus cried in agony, "My God, why hast thou forsaken me?" (Mk. 15:34b). If in our own agony of despair we do as Moses, Jeremiah, and Jesus, and address our despair to God, we shall find sympathetic understanding.

"Gluttons' Graves" was the name of this place (vv. 34-35); and, however it got its name, it was remembered as a place where some people had been more interested in good food than in obtaining liberation for their descendants. The ability of the Hebrew to criticize himself is frequently demonstrated, as it is in this story and its association with the name "Gluttons' Graves." Anyone hearing the name would be inclined to ask how the name originated. Self-criticism or evaluation is wholesome, and because the Hebrew had the capacity for self-criticism he was constantly seeking to climb to higher levels of conduct.

As noted in *ABC*, p. 302b, this chapter contains a number of fragments of tradition which are loosely woven together to make one story. This is one of the many indications we have that the writers of the biblical record were not concerned with the recording of Hebrew history, but were greatly concerned about man's conduct and about what happened to man when he failed to live in accordance with his understanding of the divine plan. This story insists that God will always aid man in getting the basic necessities of life, but that the luxuries of life must often be sacrificed in the interest of gaining greater values. This does not mean that we should never taste of the luxuries of life, but it does mean that no luxury is worth the surrender of principle.

Reading 67: Numbers 13:1-2,16–14:4

We hear frequently in these days about minority groups and reports. They are not new. The world has always had

112

them. This story is a good illustration of what faces the minority report. It is usually discarded, and often the world discovers too late that it has accepted the wrong report. All the spies reported the great advantages of the land of Canaan and the abundance of its fruit. They also agreed in the matter of the size of the cities and the strength of their defense. They were in agreement that it would be difficult to take the cities and difficult therefore to take the country. But the majority said, "It can't be taken." The minority said, "We can." The difference lay not in what they had seen but in their evaluation of themselves. Very often the difference between majority and minority reports is great. The two groups do not even observe the same things in the same way. Their different attitudes bias their reports. In this case the majority and the minority were in perfect accord until the majority reported that it was useless to think of conquering the country. As a matter of fact, they had not been asked to judge that matter. They were simply to report the strength of the camps and cities. It was the function of the commander-in-chief to judge of their ability to conquer. Caleb (13:30), and perhaps Joshua (14:5f.), believed the country could be taken.

Characteristically, the people believed the report of the majority, not because it was a majority report, but because they seemed always to accept the more pessimistic of two positions. Read what happened to Caleb later (14:24-25) and Joshua (14:7-12). Why is it that people are often more likely to believe a pessimistic rather than an optimistic report? How often fine campaigns have been ruined because a committee asked to report on one problem overstepped authority and made judgments not expected or requested from it! For example, a special committee is studying the problem of the church building. It is not suitable nor big enough for the growing church school. They are asked to report on what remodeling or building program is necessary to do a good job of education. The wise pastor will see that the report is made and that it stops with stating building needs. After the needs have been

113

made known, another committee can study resources and make recommendation as to the campaign for necessary funds. Now the church is in a position to judge whether or not it can undertake the work of a new building. But suppose the first committee had reported the needs, and then had said, "But the cost is too great; we can't raise the money." Then the church might have abandoned an opportunity. It would have done so on the basis of a statement which the committee was not qualified to make. The committee of spies was perfectly fitted to judge the strength of Canaan's defense. They had seen her cities. But they were not fitted to judge the strength of Moses' offense. Even Caleb and Joshua spoke from faith rather than from a knowledge of Moses' plan of attack. Two rules are indicated by this story: first, let us make judgments on the basis of the facts before us and let us confine our report to those facts; second, when committee reports are made, let us judge the value of the committee's report on the basis of the committee's facts. Many pessimistic reports could thereby be stopped before the church program was damaged.

Reading 68: Numbers 16:12-34

In those days men believed in a three-story universe—the regions above the firmament (which was solid), the earth itself, and the regions below. Under the earth was the place called Sheol. It was a place to which all the departed went. It was not a place where there was "life after death." Belief in a life after death came very late in O.T. writings. We read of some man, "He died and was gathered to his fathers." That was another way of saying "He has gone to Sheol." All went to the same place, good and bad alike. "Sheol," wrongly translated in the A.V. as "hell," was the place where outworn spirits were deposited. The opening to Sheol was an opening in the earth. That was the reason that all must be buried. Unless there was burial there was no way for the spirit of the departed to enter into Sheol, and the spirit must wander disconsolately over the face of the earth seeking a resting place. The same belief is found among the ancient Babylonians and the later Greeks and Romans. A sudden opening in the earth was likewise considered an opening to Sheol and was referred to as "Sheol has enlarged her mouth."

The punishment sent to these men who opposed Moses (vv. 12f., 31f.) was not their disappearance into the earth but the fact that they had been cut off from their community and from the presence of the God of Israel. Men believed in that day that they could enjoy the presence of God only here upon the earth. God had no jurisdiction over Sheol. A long life, they believed, was the reward for a good life. The description of God (vv. 28-30) is far different from the picture given in the teachings of Jesus.

The reference in v. 15 to Moses' not having take any asses from the people indicates that apparently the ass was the means of transportation in the desert at that time. The Arab of today travels by camel, but camels had not come into great use by the time of Moses. There is great difference between the ass nomad and the camel nomad. Those who travel by camel can go faster and farther than those who depend upon asses. Water holes are few in the desert, and the man who travels by ass must be sure that there is water within traveling distance before he starts on his journey. This meant slow travel, and oftentimes when good water was found travelers who used asses stayed long periods of time at the watering hole, fearing to push on with their journey. This may account for the long period that the Hebrews spent in the desert.

Reading 69: Numbers 20:14-29

The scene of this chapter is in the country of Edom south of the Dead Sea. The country was later held by the people called Nabateans. Moses asked permission to pass through on the regular caravan route and indicated his willingness to pay for water. Permission was not granted, and of necessity the Hebrews changed their route, going far to the south in order to go around the country they could not go through. Recent archaeological investigations indicate that this journey of the Hebrews must have been in the twelfth century B.C. It could not have been earlier for the simple reasons that in the earlier centuries there were no settled people in any strength in this territory and it would not have been necessary to ask permission to go through. Here is more evidence for dating Moses in the twelfth century.

The phrase asking permission (v. 17) is similar to that sent to the king of the Amorites (21:21-22). It indicates settled communities having cultivated fields and vineyards. Few, if any, are known in that part of the land today. The phrase suggests that Moses was ready to promise that his people would not steal grain, cattle, or fruit. It may have been the fear of the Edomite king that Moses would not be successful in his attempt to keep the Hebrews from plundering the territory that caused the king to refuse permission. Wanderers had a reputation as plunderers. They still are feared, and frequently sweep into settled communities to steal and plunder. The king of Edom had the responsibility to protect his own people.

The death of Aaron is told for the twofold purpose of completing the story of the rebellion at the waters of Meribah (20:2-13) and indicating also the succession of the priesthood. The loss of Aaron must have been a great one to the Israelites, but their grief is passed over quickly by this writer, except to state that they mourned his death thirty days (see *ABC*, p. 308f.). Eleazar now has become the great priest and has been clothed in the robes of his office. His appearance in camp wearing these robes must have been the signal to the people that Aaron was dead (vv. 28-29). Yet, perhaps the priest who records this event is indicating that the people of Israel held the priesthood in high regard because of the man Aaron who had served so long and so well in that office. Succession to any office is not important or desired unless the office is one of good reputation. That reputation is established by those who have held the office. The office of priest was one of honor in Israel, at least in the early days, and Aaron was one of the men who brought this honor to the office of priesthood.

116

Reading 70: Numbers 22:2-38

This delightful collection of stories concerning Balaam's ass is in true Oriental pattern. These stories grew up as the years passed, beginning with short anecdotes and having more details added as the stories were retold. The detailed analysis is given in *ABC*, pp. 309f.

V. 4 gives a perfectly natural setting. The Moabites were afraid of the plundering habits of wandering nomads such as the Israelites. The Moabites could not stop the Hebrews with force, but the king thought that they might be stopped by a religious curse. Blessings and curses were frequently used for national purposes in those days. Balaam, son of Beor, had a great reputation for powerful blessings and cursings. Balaam at first refused to go, but finally agreed to go and to speak only what he felt that God wanted him to say. One is reminded of the old Babylonian king who desired to march against his enemies but dared not go without knowing that he had the blessing of his god. He therefore ordered his priest to consult the oracle and receive that blessing. But the priest reported that the god did not permit the king to fight this particular enemy. The priest was immediately ordered to inquire again, but the result was the same. The answer of the god was "No." The Babylonian king said, "There must be a mistake, consult the god again." This time the priest obtained the right answer, permission to march out in battle. The king answered triumphantly, "You see, I go with the blessing of God, and at his request." King Balak desired but one answer from Balaam, namely, a curse upon the Hebrews. Balaam's reply (vv. 18-19) is testimony to his honesty and sincerity.

The contradiction between vv. 20 and 22 is startling. The first gives permission to go, but the second indicates the anger of God because he went.

An ass speaking with human voice disturbs the modern Western mind. The Oriental, ancient and modern, delights in this form of behavior in his stories. He is not a literalist as we are. If animals serve his purpose in telling his stories,

117

he uses them. Animals were thought also to have quicker perception of the supernatural than man. Thus the ass sensed the presence of the angel before his master.

The emphasis in this story is on the fact that Balaam could not be persuaded nor hired to say anything that he believed contrary to the will of God. Of course, there is the further underlying teaching that no one in any nation could bring harm to God's people. This conviction that Israel was chosen and blessed of God is persistent from earliest times, and is strong in Judaism today. What does it mean to be "God's people"? Israel's difficulty came when the nation refused to face moral responsibility but expected divine blessing.

Reading 71: Numbers 25:1-15

One of the most bitter fights in religious history was the struggle between Baalism and the religion of Jehovah. Baalism used a form of imitation magic. The people believed that if they imitated an act which they desired the gods to perform they could force the gods through magic to do man's bidding. In this chapter such magic plays its part. Mock marriage by the people symbolized the union of the Baal of growth with Mother Earth, which union was supposed to insure the growth of vegetation and animal life. Against this religion the prophets fought hard and long and were finally victorious. There were many things wrong with this view of religion and life. Its first fault was that its emphasis was upon material prosperity. The great purpose of the Baal religion was to make things grow more quickly and better. The second fault was that it taught that the right religious magic "persuaded" the gods to do what man desired. We have discovered that one great principle of religion must be to bring life into harmony with the great purposes of God, not to try to bend God to man's will or use him for man's ends. That is what Jesus meant when he taught his disciples to pray "Thy will be done." Finally, the temporary union of men and women was recognized by the prophets as licentious, and the use

118

of great amounts of wine at these Baal festivals led to conduct that was bestial. It can easily be seen why men were converted to the Baal religion, and why it was so difficult to remove it from Israel's desires.

V. 6 brings a new situation and is abruptly introduced. The Midianites lived far to the south of the Edomites and east of the Red Sea, in a country which which is now inhabited by Arabs. The offense is not clear, but apparently marriage with a foreigner was not tolerated. The anger of the people was aroused when the man brought the foreign woman within sight of the leaders and people at a time of religious ceremonial. Immediately Phinehas slew the man and the woman. The people believed that the man and the woman had caused the disease that was plaguing Israel and that the people had been saved by the quick action of Phinehas. V. 9 indicates that twenty-four thousand people had died from the disease. Men believed that punishment came quickly and directly from God when men sinned, and that the punishment was severe. It came upon the whole group because the Covenant was between the group and God. That is why the group so often killed men who were judged guilty of sin. It was the only way they knew how to keep the community purged of sin. Death or expulsion immediately removed sinners and uncleanness. It was more important for them that Phinehas had cleaned out rottenness from God's people than that he had taken human life. The descendants of Phinehas were rewarded by becoming a family of priests. This is hardly according to Christian standards. We believe that men become ministers of God because of their own religious experiences and convictions, and because of individual fitness, not because they belong to certain families, or because of the deeds of their ancestors.

Reading 72: Numbers 27:1-23

It had been the custom in Israel that when a man died his estate was inherited by his nearest male kin. Woman had no place in the rights of inheritance. This chapter is one of the latest portions of the book of Numbers to be written, and indicates that within the memory of the writer had come the change making it possible for a daughter to gain possession of her father's estate. Ch. 36 provides that while a daughter may take possession of the property left by her father, she must marry within the tribal group so as to preserve the property to the tribe. Deut. 21:15f. and 25:5-10 recognize only sons as heirs. It is probable that women did not gain their property rights until the post-exilic period (after 538 B.C.). V. 1 indicates that there had been no law regarding such matters, and that it came into existence only when an actual problem was presented to the leaders. That is always the history of Law, whether religious or civil.

The closing part of the chapter tells of Moses and his preparation of a successor. "Invest him with some of your own majesty" (v. 20—American Trans.). Does this mean that Joshua would receive greater respect from the community if it were known that Moses approved of him as a leader? Perhaps. Does it mean that Joshua needed to catch something of the spirit of Moses by association with him? Or was it external authority that Moses was to give to Joshua? Certainly the power of Moses came from the character of the man. His followers knew that he was sincere, and that he was a man of deep convictions. They knew above all that he was a man of God. Joshua became a majestic personality when Israel discovered these same things in him.

The remainder of the book of Numbers is concerned with many items, but most of them are of little interest to us today. The closing chapters consist of lists of offerings, camp sites, vows, settlement of various tribes, boundaries, and the special cities set aside for refuge. (See *ABC*, pp. 313-17.)

Written Work.—Write a sermon on "Courage," using Moses, Caleb, Joshua, and Balaam for illustration. What was the source of their courage? Is courage a Christian virtue? Do we need it today? Where?

VIII

LAW INSPIRED BY PROPHECY
Deuteronomy 1–26

IN 2 Kings, chs. 22-23, the story is told of finding a "Book of Law," at the time of the repair of the Temple in 621 B.C. King Joshua immediately reformed the religious practices in Jerusalem and in Judea on the basis of this newly found law. It is now generally agreed by scholars that the document found in the Temple has been preserved, and is the same as chs. 12-26 and ch. 28 of Deuteronomy. Read *ABC,* pp. 92f. and 318-22. In all probability the "Code" had been written not very long before its discovery in the walls of the Temple. We should like to know exactly who wrote this law. Note that Huldah the prophetess did not say who had written it, nor when it was written (see 2 Kings 22:15-17). Her statement was simply that if the people lived in accordance with the teaching of this law, they would be living in harmony with God's will. Careful comparison of these laws with the teachings of the great prophets of the eighth century B.C. indicates that the laws came as the result of these teachings. Some men had heard the prophets and were inspired by their messages. They asked themselves how they could put these messages into the lives of people. They realized that men needed some rules to live by, and that the nation needed great laws founded upon the laws of God. The book of Deuteronomy is an excellent example of putting religious teaching into daily life. There were many additions to the original law in the years that followed. Chs. 1-11, 27, and 29-34 are all part of the later writings. It was in the later period, after the Exile, that Jews began to say that all Law had come through Moses; and that thought has been repeated down to the present time in spite of the fact that there is no statement in the book of Deuteronomy that attributes all law to Moses. Much law came from Moses, but new needs and new experiences demanded new law, and this new law was added to the ever increasing "Law of Moses."

The book of Deuteronomy differs so considerably from the other portions of the Books of Law that these differences are worth noting. There is an emphasis throughout this book on the love of God and man's responding love. This note in religion was not sounded until Hosea began to teach in the eighth century B.C. There are strong indications, too, that this book was never considered a formal codification of law. In the first place, these laws are worded as a preacher would word them, not as a lawyer would. There is constant exhortation to the people to live up to the ideals set forth in these laws. Note also that there are no penalties named for the violation of specific laws, such as are regularly included in formal legislation.

The results of the reform in Judah that was inspired by this Book of Law were both good and bad. On the good side there was a general denunciation of the Baal religion and an attempt to raise the standards by which men lived. There was centralization of power, both political and religious, in Jerusalem. This may have been good or bad. One of the bad results was that religion now tended to be fixed. Religious standards and teachings were now recorded in a book and could not be changed. The answers to all religious questions had been written down, and little room was left for new religious experiences. This is one of the things that led to the decline of prophetic activity in the period after the Exile, and the growth toward Pharisaism. The greatest result of this newly discovered book was its acceptance by the people and its recognition as Scripture. The book of Deuteronomy was the first book in history to be accounted as Scripture. It was around this book that the Hebrews began to gather those books now known to us as the Bible. That is why the book of Deuteronomy is so important and so worthy of our attention and study. This book is the greatest attempt of the Hebrew people to climb to the high challenge of the prophets. They never quite reached the ideal of the prophets, nor their own ideals, but at least they said, "This is what we should like to be." The challenge still holds. It is from this book that the Jews wrote their great creed. It was from this book that Jesus quoted the great summary of religion.

Reading 73: Deuteronomy 1:1-18

The introduction to the book (chs. 1-4) indicates that the record was written later than the time of Moses (1:1-5). (Cf. 4:41-43, 44-49; 5:1; 27:1, 9, 11; 29:1; 31:1f.; and 34:1f.) The speeches of Moses are given in which the history of the wanderings is reviewed. The book does not say who the compiler is, but we are greatly indebted to him for gathering together these traditions regarding the early days of the Hebrew people.

V. 6 is a revealing picture of the Hebrews. They were content to settle down wherever it was convenient. Frequently they forgot the great goal. They needed to be prodded into action. The message now is "Move on." Great goals and great leadership are not enough. The people of God must move forward if the objectives are to be reached.

In vv. 9-18 we have a retelling of the story of the choice of division leaders in Israel (cf. Ex. 18:21 and Num. 11:16-17). In this case Moses is represented as making the suggestion himself. He may have made the proposal to the people following his father-in-law's advice. The qualifications are worth comparing with those suggested in Ex. 18:21 (review *Reading* 39). These leaders are to be chosen. They must be capable, intelligent, and experienced men (v. 13). Intelligence is a necessary part of capability. Experience will guide the leader to wise decisions and will give him greater balance in judgment. Other qualifications are noted in v. 17. The leader must be impartial. This was particularly true here, for the primary responsibility of these leaders was to act as judges. Justice is dependent upon

123

an impartial weighing of the evidence. We usually think of justice as being completely in the hands of elected or appointed judges who have been trained in law. But in the modern world, judgment and justice are more often in the hands of citizens. The evidence is presented in court and a judge presides over the courtroom, but it is a group of citizens in the jury box that determines guilt or innocence. These jurymen must weigh evidence impartially and refuse to be swayed by the emotional appeals of the prosecuting or defending attorneys. Each juryman has a moral responsibility to make an impartial judgment, and in his capacity as juryman he is a leader and represents his fellow citizens to see that justice is done.

Further, Moses indicated that justice should be available to all, the high and the low (v. 17), the resident and the alien, the employer and the employee (v. 16). In the modern world it is often an expensive process to conduct a lawsuit, or to have adequate defense when one is accused of a crime. What are the provisions in your community to see that justice is available to all men regardless of their economic condition or the color of their skin? Is there not an obligation upon us as Christians to see that these ancient principles of Moses are applied to our present society? Put in your notebook the ways in which we carry out Moses' principles today. A final characteristic is suggested for Moses' aides. They are to fear no man, remembering that true justice is from God. Does this mean that the man who sees that justice is done, whether he be judge or juryman, is an agent of God?

Reading 74: Deuteronomy 4:15-43

The Hebrews are reminded in this passage that God is a spirit, or at least that he cannot be seen by mankind. They are reminded, too, that they can be aware of communion with God. During their history they were to come in contact with many neighbors, each of whom had his own representations of his gods. Some portrayed them in human form, as in Baalism. Birds and animals symbolized the gods of Egypt and Phoenicia. The fish has been associated with the Philistine god Dagon (though it is known that Dagon was a god of grain). The Babylonians, then the Assyrians, worshiped the sun, moon, and stars; and at one time symbols of the "chariots of the sun" were installed at the Temple in Jerusalem. (See 2 Kings 23:11-12.) All such representations kept the concept of God on a low level. The Hebrews fought constantly to prevent the making of images to represent the Deity. They were not always successful. (See 1 Kings 12:28-29 and Deut. 4:27-28.)

They are reminded (vv. 23f.) that in the Covenant relationship they have a special responsibility. There was a widespread practice of leaving all responsibility to God and forgetting that man must assume his share.

The nearness of God is stressed in vv. 29-31. With the growing emphasis that there is only one God, many men came to think of God as far removed from the earth and not easily available to man. This is one of the problems that face men today. How can the great Creator of our enormous universe be aware of mere men and their little needs? The Hebrews said through their national experience, "God *is* aware." The prophets and other men since their day have shared in this conviction because of their personal experiences. List in your notebook ways in which we may be aware of the presence of God. The psalms offer many suggestions. Would this theme make a good sermon?

Vv. 34-40 assert again that God had a destiny for the Hebrew people and that the reverses by Egypt or any other power could not prevent that purpose from accomplishment. Other nations have had a similar conviction, though perhaps not quite in the same sense. For any nation to say, "We are God's people," can lead to good or to evil. If that nation believes that God will bless them to the exclusion of others, that is selfishness; but if they believe that through them a mission to the world may be accomplished, then the belief can lead to much good.

The three cities set aside (vv. 41-43) were known as Levitical cities (see Num. 35:6f., where six cities are listed), or cities of refuge. These cities were designated as places of protection for an accused man. The earlier practice seems to have been to hold the horns of the altar (Ex. 21:12-14). See *ABC,* p. 75, and Josh. 20. Before courts were established, or formal procedure in law, it was often difficult for an accused man to escape the vengeance of his accusers. A life taken demanded another life as penalty. Blood revenge was swift, but not always just. To provide for a "cooling-off period," places of sanctuary were established. This meant that there was time for tempers to cool, and for a man to state his defense, while the accused was in a city of refuge. Here was another step in the direction of justice.

Reading 75: Deuteronomy 5:1-33

Read carefully the notes in *ABC,* pp. 325-26, regarding this chapter. Notations are made there of the differences between this version of the Ten Commandments and that found in Ex. 20.

The Sabbath is considered a divine institution for the benefit of man. In Exodus it is stated that the Sabbath was created because God first had need of it. In Deuteronomy nothing is said of God's resting, but rest is to be given to all men and women, including servants, to remind the Hebrews that they once had been slaves in Egypt.

Note that throughout this version of the commandments the status of woman is definitely improved. Compare v. 21 with Ex. 20:17; Deut. 21:10f.; 22:13f.; 24:1.

The latter part of the chapter is concerned with the mediation of Moses between God and the people. There is fear expressed by the people as they became aware of divine power. It is the age-old cry of man, who believes that there are certain individuals who are more acceptable to the Deity than is the ordinary man. This is one basis of priest-craft. In Protestantism we have insisted upon the priesthood of all believers, but it must not be forgotten that it is expected that the minister shall know the way to God as well as any man, and better than most. The Protestant minister is a leader in the church because he has discovered the values of religion and the companionship of God and seeks to lead others into that fellowship. His message is one that begins with personal testimony. It is his privilege, as well as his responsibility, to lead other men along the path of discovery.

Reading 76: Deuteronomy 6: 1-25

Here is the heart of Hebrew religious practice and belief. Vv. 4-9 have been recited by the Jews for centuries as their creed, or statement of belief. It asserts their conviction that there is only one God. The world is forever indebted to the Hebrews for this magnificent teaching. They alone of the ancient peoples believed this great truth. The creed does not stop with stating the central fact of their faith, but goes on to state how this teaching shall be kept alive. Their religious education began with the children. Children shall be taught the religious Law. The implication of the verses that follow is that the teaching shall be the responsibility of the home. The Hebrews are instructed to talk about these things constantly—in the home, in the morning, and at night—and there are to be constant reminders of the centralities of their faith. There shall be symbols on the hand and forehead, and on the gates and doorposts of the home. It is probable that these words were not intended to be taken literally, but they have been so interpreted by later Jews. By the time of Jesus, Jews were wearing little boxes strapped to their hands and foreheads when they attended religious services. These boxes contained passages of Scripture. Similarly, the Jewish home had a symbol on the doorpost, or doorframe, not to mark the home as Jewish, but to remind the members of the family that the faith of their fathers is the faith in that home. What is the value of such daily reminders? Is this better than being reminded of our faith only when we attend church on Sunday? A Japanese Christian said: "In every Japanese home there is a little corner containing the emblems of religion. In each Catholic home I see pictures

127

or symbols of their faith. But when I go into a Protestant home I cannot tell whether it is Christian or not." We shall say immediately that Christianity consists not in symbols but in the way one lives. Nevertheless, is it not true that so often we have been ashamed to have outward evidences of faith about us?

The home was made responsible for the religious instruction of children. Does this account for the tenacity of Hebrew religious culture? Many people believe so. There is a problem that faces us in this method of teaching in the home. Religion is an intimately personal matter. Many men find it difficult to talk to their children and their wives about religion. They find it easier to talk to a stranger. Religion should become so truly a part of our lives that we can talk about it as naturally as we live it. Is religion really alive unless it is expressed in our daily homelife? Is religion important if it exists only in the things we do and say at church and Sunday school? What is the attitude of the child who is told that he must get the answers to his religious questions at the church? Will there not be a tendency for the child whose parents stay at home while he goes to Sunday school to look forward to the day when he can be an adult and forget about religion? Put in your notebooks a statement as to the division of responsibility for religious education between the home and the church.

Reading 77: Deuteronomy 7:1-16

Annihilate! No compromise! These were the cries raised by leaders of the Hebrews. They were not always obeyed, but the leaders recognized that there was great danger in mingling too freely with people of strange customs and beliefs. These cries against intermarriage and intermingling grew louder as the years went by. History demonstrated that the few were right when they said the Hebrews should have no dealings with the seven nations named in v. 1. At the time of the entry of the Hebrews into the land of Palestine the religion of the Hebrews was virtually new. Under the guidance of Moses they had accepted Jehovah as

God, but many times there were those who desired to return to the place and beliefs of Egypt. The time of greatest danger in any religious movement is in its beginning, for it is then that it is most easily influenced by others. Marriage between members of different religious faiths also presents great difficulty, even where the man and woman are members of different branches of the same religion. The new bride and groom are strange in each other's presence at first. Perhaps each has learned different religious practices and hesitates to embarrass the other. Too often the final result is that each one gives up his religious practices, and there is no religion in the home. In ancient Palestine the stronger of the two would be likely to survive. Since the practices of the Hittites and others were well established, and their shrines were to be seen in many places, the newcoming religion of the Hebrews would have a difficult time.

The altars, sacred pillars, sacred poles, and carved images in v. 5 were symbols of the enemy religion. The Hebrews knew that if the religions of their enemies were to be rooted out they must destroy those symbols. The "Asherim" were sacred poles emblematic of Baal religion, just as the cross is the emblem of the Christian Church.

V. 13 gives a picture of Jehovah different from the conception the Hebrews had in the desert. There they were concerned with God's leadership in danger. They had associated God with the mountains, and particularly with the storms of the mountain. As the Hebrews moved into Palestine they had to know whether the God of agriculture was Baal, as claimed by the Canaanites, or whether Jehovah could take care of their new farming activities. This verse asserts that God will give them the very things that Baalism claimed for its religion. It is difficult for us to think of any limitation on the powers of God, but in that day men associated different gods with different countries and different powers. Actually, each was thinking of but one phase of the nature and power of God. It was necessary for men to come together and compare their ideas before

129

they could get a greater concept of the nature of God. For the Hebrews to come in contact with the Canaanites, Hittites, and others, made them ask why men believed differently, and whether the Hebrews themselves or their opponents were right. It is good for man to have his ideas challenged occasionally so that he may discover why he believes as he does. In this way, also, man's knowledge grows through contact with new knowledge.

Reading 78: Deuteronomy 8:5-20

There is peril in prosperity! To say, "My own power and the strength of my own hand have gained this wealth for me," is a temptation into which many men and nations fall. Put into modern terms, this writer's thought is: "When prosperity comes to you, remember these things. The strength you use comes from God. The great treasures that you mine were placed there not by you but by the Creator. The productivity of your fields is due not to your wisdom but to the creative power of God. The wealth with which you have purchased your fine homes and the luxuries upon your table is from God. You ought to be grateful to God and to express your thanks." The hardest men in society to persuade of their need of religion are those who have been economically successful and perhaps refer to themselves as "self-made men." They have wealth, position, power, prestige, and are tempted to believe that money can give them whatever they desire. If there is illness they can afford the finest specialists. If there is conflict with other men regarding property or personal rights they can afford the best legal advice. Some such men have even had local or state laws enacted for their special benefit. They believe that it is sometimes necessary to pay, but not to pray. Of course, this is assuming that the main function of prayer is petition, especially in times of disaster or frustration. But v. 10 reminds us that a large element of religion must be thanksgiving. The man who recognizes God as the giver of all will save himself from an exaggerated sense of his own importance. The man or woman who is truly thankful and recognizes the source of blessings will derive greater happiness from life than will those who do not.

We must go beyond the thought of v. 18, however, where it expresses the idea that power to make wealth is given to the Hebrews because God has promised it to their ancestors. The message of Jesus has added the thought that there is a trusteeship in life. Power and wealth are to be used only for the good of all, certainly not to the detriment of others.

Once more (vv. 19-20) there is warning not to forget God and not to turn to other religions. History demonstrates that those nations that have become self-sufficient and have left the leaven of religion out of their national and individual lives have ultimately gone down to destruction. List in your notebook the dangers that face men as prosperity comes to them, and also what principles should be followed in using one's material possessions.

Reading 79: Deuteronomy 9:6-29

Here is an old story rewritten to counsel the people and to portray the magnificent work of Moses (see Ex. 32:1-35). The writer stresses (v. 6) that the success of the Hebrews will be due to the graciousness of God, not to the goodness of the people. After summarizing the old story and adding some details (see vv. 20-21), he continues with an emphasis upon the agony of Moses when he interceded on behalf of the people. The account of Moses agonizing before the Lord for many days and of his pleas in their behalf is one of the outstanding religious pictures of all time. The expression "forty days" is the regular Hebrew phrase meaning a long period, not an exact measurement of time. The emphasis is not upon the time but upon the intensity of the prayer and the devotion of Moses to God and to his people. This prayer is intensely personal. What does it mean to a people to know that their leader has offered this kind of prayer in their behalf? Contrast this with the formal prayer that is often associated with religious obligation, as when the priest in Israel presented certain specified offerings and prayers.

131

There are two factors involved in a situation of this kind. First, the character of the individual who is praying must be above reproach in the eyes of those for whom he petitions. It is a great tribute to the love that Israel had for Moses that this story of his career was so well remembered. Second, the people are touched because the problem involves them so intimately and personally. Tell a man that you have prayed for him and in all probability, if he has respect and regard for you, he will be so emotionally moved that he will scarcely be able to respond in words. One of the great opportunities of a pastor is that of being able to pray for his people. Should such prayer be confined to the pastor? Is there danger that men in praying for others will become self-righteous? How can we guard against that danger? Is there anything in this story of Moses to indicate a sense of superiority?

V. 29 stresses again the conviction that the Hebrews are God's people because God has made them his own by his deliverance of them as a nation. The Christian idea goes far beyond this when it says that God has a purpose for all mankind and that he does not fight against one people for the benefit of another.

Reading 80: Deuteronomy 10:3-22

The Ark of the Covenant was an important piece of furniture in the early Hebrew tent of meeting and tabernacle (see Num. 10:33). According to tradition it contained the tables of Law and symbolized the Covenant relation between Jehovah and the Hebrews. The Ark signified the presence of God in their midst. It was borne in procession to indicate the leadership of God in their journeys. It was carried about Jericho at the time of the taking of that city (Josh. 6:4-12). The Philistines took it from the Hebrews (1 Sam. 4:3-11); it was returned because of fear (1 Sam. 5:7). Finally it was taken to Jerusalem (2 Sam. 6:1-19), and later it was installed in the Temple of Solomon (1 Kings 8:6-9). The Ark may have been replaced by the great altar of Ahaz (2 Kings 16:10-18), or it may have been destroyed at the time of the Babylonian invasion.

Vv. 8-9 are inserted to explain the office of the Levite. (See *Reading* 65.)

In v. 16 a plea is made that the people will receive the spirit of God. They have been more concerned about the ritualistic observance of the Law of Moses than its spirit. The rite of circumcision has been performed with great ceremony for many centuries. It marks a man as a Jew, and this "mark in the flesh" has been recognized as one of the signs of the Covenant. The writer now pleads that men's hearts will likewise be marked with the sign of God. This is the very thing for which the prophet Jeremiah pleads (Jer. 4:4; 9:26).

Read carefully vv. 17-18. This great portrayal of the character of God is difficult to surpass. It sets up an ideal for man also. To be impartial and to have a concern for the unfortunate in society was an ideal that came into the Hebrew consciousness as a result of the teachings of the great prophets Amos, Hosea, Isaiah, and Jeremiah.

God is to be the object of the nation's praise, for God has done marvellous things in history (vv. 20-22). In particular, he has made a great nation, Israel, out of seventy people who went down into Egypt.

Reading 81: Deuteronomy 12:1-19

We turn now to the heart of the book of Deuteronomy. Chs. 12-26 contain the core of the Law of Israel. These chapters may be grouped in four divisions: (1) 12:1–16:17, laws of worship and obligations to God; (2) 16:18–18:22, laws concerning various ecclesiastical and civil officials; (3) 19:1–21:9, laws relating to crime, war, property, and evidence; (4) chs. 22-25, miscellaneous laws relating to civil, personal, and military problems; ch. 26 is an appendix.

This Law Code begins with the assumption that the community is primarily a religious one. There are civil problems involved, but the constitution proceeds from the basic assumption that God is the chief ruler of the people and that the people are subject to him in all of their activity. Absolute obedience is enjoined, and all symbols or sacred places that would detract from loyalty to Jehovah are to be obliterated.

The opening verses also contain one of the main assertions of this code (vv. 5, 13-14)—that there is to be one central place of worship for the Hebrews. It is not identified here, but it is clear from this and other writings that Jerusalem is meant. This was part of the Deuteronomic reform under Josiah. The dominant aim and interest of Deuteronomy was the purification of worship and the elimination of ancient local cults with their local gods and low ideals. The reform was carried forward zealously, and wayside shrines of the other religions in Palestine were torn down. Attention was directed toward Jerusalem as a religious and political center. There were two great problems that resulted from this removal of local places of worship. First, it meant that there were few times when many of the people could go to a place of worship. Jerusalem was a long way off for most of them. There was no local place of worship to which they could turn in times of need. The problem was much like that in the parable told by Jesus of the man whose mind was unoccupied after evil had been driven out, and whose last condition was worse than the first (Mt. 12:43-45). Here, also, evil was not replaced with good but a vacancy was left, and in the end the Hebrew people were in a very bad situation.

The second difficulty was that, with the priests being driven out of the small towns and wayside places, the people centered in Jerusalem and began to compete for position and power. It may have been this that led Jeremiah to react so violently against the priesthood of his day. (See Jer. 6:13-15; 8:8-12.) The Hebrew people learned through bitter experience two lessons. When people are left without constant spiritual guidance and inspiration their moral standards become progressively worse. One means of offsetting this handicap of centralization of worship was the establishment, in the postexilic period, of the synagogue.

The synagogue began as a place of religious instruction, but because of the needs of people it soon became the equivalent of a local church, or place of worship. The second lesson was that when the spiritual leaders, the priests and prophets, fail in their responsibilities and moral conduct, the community also fails. The Hebrews knew no answer to this problem except that leaders and people must keep close to God.

Written Work.—Make an outline of the ways in which a religious leader may teach religion in addition to his regular sermons or Sunday school lessons. Show specifically how men learn the values of a religious life by watching a genuinely religious man.

Reading 82: Deuteronomy 12:20-32

Meat is always a luxury in and around Palestine. It is hard to procure, and usually a family fortunate enough to have meat invites in its friends and relatives. In ancient times, also, it was customary to consider all eating of meat a religious festival to be performed only in the presence of the God. With centralization of all religious ceremonials at Jerusalem the Hebrews were confronted with a problem. It was not possible to take all animals and all those who would partake of the meal up to Jerusalem. It therefore became the custom to take the great sacrificial offerings to Jerusalem, and to observe the lesser religious acts at home. There was a distinct attempt also to break the old custom of considering all meat eating a religious act. Only in this way could they keep an emphasis upon the central place of the Holy City. The regulation given here distinctly says that the people were permitted to eat meat whenever they desired (v. 20) but that they were required to eat it as an ordinary, not a sacrificial, meal (v. 22).

There was still the obligation, however, to see that the meat was kosher, that is, that the animal was one of those recognized as clean food and that all blood was drained from the flesh. These were the chief requirements of kosher. Other regulations included the manner in which

135

the animal was killed, so that there would be no mistake about the complete draining of the blood, and the proper person to do the killing. Today, kosher meat is prepared only by a person authorized by the Jewish synagogue or temple, and that person must be ritualistically clean at the time he slays the animal. So important has this feature of Jewish religion become that slaughterhouses employ special persons for the preparation of kosher meat, and this food is sold in special markets.

The final warning of this passage is that the Hebrews are not to copy religious customs of other peoples. This goes beyond the previous admonition to refrain from turning to other gods; this prohibits the adoption of customs from foreign religions, however attractive or enticing the customs might be. The effect of this warning was to make the people do their own religious thinking. They were encouraged to develop religious customs in answer to their own needs and according to the teachings of their own religion, not simply to adopt some custom because other people seemed to "get something out of it." One of the reasons for the violent hatred the Hebrews had for the religious practices of other people is the fact, as indicated in v. 31, that they still practiced human sacrifice.

Reading 83: Deuteronomy 13:1-18

This chapter sets forth three groups of people who might be instrumental in changing the loyalty of the Hebrew people: the prophets, loved ones, and scoundrels. Warning is severe that the Hebrews should be influenced by none of these.

The prophets referred to here are not to be identified with such men as Amos or Isaiah. They were men who made their fortunes by interpreting dreams or giving signs. There were many of them in the country and the warning was necessary. Death was the penalty decreed for such an individual.

The members of one's family are the most difficult to

136

oppose in many ways. Particularly is this true when those individuals say, "We have tried this new way and it works." Jesus said that the members of a man's own household could be his enemies (Mt. 10:36). Jesus therefore taught that it was necessary sometimes to turn against one's family if remaining with them would result in compromise in one's standards or conduct. Jesus differed from Deuteronomy in that he said we should leave such people and be independent of them. Deuteronomy demanded the death of such individuals. The death penalty was to be imposed by stoning. The man to cast the first stone was the man who first witnessed that the culprit was seeking to corrupt the Hebrew religion. The effect of this last provision undoubtedly was to limit the number of charges and convictions. Perhaps it was this same passage that Jesus had in mind when he suggested that the individual without sin should cast the first stone at the woman taken in adultery (John 8:7).

Those of the last group are actually called scoundrels (vv. 12-18). They are to be dealt with just as severely. The warning to beware of such individuals was well taken, for often the attitude of well-meaning people is that since they know certain groups or individuals are bad they are therefore warned and need take no further note of them. This passage indicates that we have a responsibility for those to whom they are doing harm. Evil is to be ruthlessly rooted out of the community.

In none of the cases was it suggested that these people in turn might be converted to the Hebrew position. The Hebrews have never been a missionary-minded or evangelistic people. It was left to Christianity to become the great crusading religion with the message that God is concerned for all people and the way of salvation is open to all. Compare the provisions of this chapter for the ruthless extermination of all who did not believe as the Hebrews did with the message of Jesus that men are to be won through love, for a God who loves them.

137

Reading 84: Deuteronomy 14:1-2, 21–15:6

The beginning of this chapter is concerned with special phases of the worship of the dead. Cutting oneself was more than an act of mourning. It was a type of self-sacrifice on behalf of the departed. Compare 1 Kings 18:28, where the Baal worshipers gashed themselves and let their blood flow in order to revive their god Baal. Shaving between the eyes was another act connected with the worship of the dead. Read *ABC*, p. 330.

Anything that died a natural death was not to be eaten. Compare Ex. 22:31, where such provision is made only for an animal that died in combat. This regulation was not concerned with how the animal died or any poison that might come from eating it. In fact it is stated that such animals could be sold to foreigners or given to aliens, since they had no religious scruples.

The religious dues were to be carefully computed. If the family lived far from Jerusalem it was permissible to sell the grain or animals, and to take the money obtained to Jerusalem. Note, however, that when the worshiper arrived at Jerusalem he was to purchase offerings with this money and then proceed with his sacrificial offerings and act as if he had transported the animals there.

Two further provisions are made in this passage. Every third year money enough is to be taken out of the religious offerings to provide for necessitous cases at home. Compare that with the attitude of many modern churches who reverse the process and keep most of the money at home and send only a little for work elsewhere. Those to be cared for include the alien among the Hebrews (v. 29).

Provision is made also for the periodical canceling of debts. This is the background of the custom in some states and countries that after a certain length of time debts are legally outlawed. The insistence was that there were to be no poor people among the Hebrews. This is a policy that has been followed by the Jews whenever humanly possible. The Jews, today, are renowned for their program of relief among their own people, and for their generosity to others. Above the doorway of the National Jewish Hospital, Denver, are inscribed these words: "None may enter who can pay, none can pay who enters." Throughout the years this hospital has admitted more Gentiles than Jews. They have believed that God blesses generosity.

Reading 85: Deuteronomy 15:7-23

Two more regulations are now made for the treatment of the poor and the slave (vv. 7-11, 12-18). The plea of the poor must always be heard, and the Hebrews are warned not to refuse to aid them. This legislation recognizes that it will be easy to refuse aid on the basis that the poor will quickly be eligible for relief from public funds or the outlawing of debt by the lapse of time.

Second, there is provision for the release of the slave after six years of service (cf. Ex. 21:2-6). The statement in v. 18 that a man who has worked for six years in slavery has worked at half cost may have reference to the Babylonian practice of liberation after three years. See the comment in *Reading* 41. It may also reflect the economic pattern, in which a slave's labor was considered worth only half as much as that of a free man.

There is here also a use of history for teaching purposes, not simply to indicate the way in which God has blessed the nation and has carried out his great purposes, but to remind the Hebrew constantly of his former condition of slavery. To the people of Jesus' day, who were very familiar with this use of history, the parable of the ungrateful servant (Mt. 18:22-35) must have had great significance. Jesus was simply reminding the people through a well-told illustration of a truth that was already known to them.

The old law of the consecration to God of the firstlings of the flocks and herds is rewritten here (cf. Ex. 13:11-16). The old practice was to leave the newly-born animal with its dam for eight days (Ex. 22:28), then to offer it as sacrifice. Here provision is made for keeping the animal longer. This was undoubtedly due to the fact of centralization of

139

worship at Jerusalem, whereas in an earlier day the people offered sacrifice wherever they happened to be. However, injunction is made against using this consecrated animal for work. It belonged to God and could not be used for human benefit. If there was blemish of any kind on the animal, it could be eaten as regular food. Only perfect animals could be offered in sacrifice. The later provisions of Num. 18:15-18, written during the days of a highly developed priesthood, give the first-born animals to the priesthood. No such privilege is granted in the writings of Deuteronomy (18:1-8).

Each of these provisions seems to keep three standards uppermost in the minds of the people. Conduct before God was to be irreproachable, in daily life and at the offering of sacrifices. Religious practices were made to conform to the conditions under which men lived. Man must be concerned about his fellow man, for he must never forget that in his own need God was gracious to him.

The individual Hebrew identified himself with the experiences of the whole nation. He was taught to think of himself not as an exception but as one of a people who had been in a condition of suffering and slavery. This teaching stressed the everlasting dependence of man upon God.

Reading 86: Deuteronomy 16:1–17:1

Not only are the ceremonials of religion centered in Jerusalem, but Deuteronomy also provides that at the time of the three great religious festivals all men shall journey to Jerusalem for the celebration. The three great feasts are the Passover (vv. 1-8), the Feast of Weeks (vv. 9-12), and the Feast of Booths (vv. 13-15).

The provision for all men to attend these festivals was not to exclude the women. It was based on the old patriarchal pattern of society, with its belief that all property was owned by the men and therefore all offerings were rightly made by them, not by the family. It meant that the emphasis of religion was still upon the offering of sacri-

140

fices and the payment of dues, not upon the help that religion could give in daily living.

The Passover, or Feast of Unleavened Bread, was held for seven days in March or April. The time was fixed by the phase of the moon, not the anniversary of a specific date. The Christian date for Easter depends still upon the Jewish custom of fixing the Passover. There are a number of churches, also, that use unleavened bread in the sacrament of the Lord's Supper. Many scholars now believe that Jesus did not eat the Passover with his disciples, but ate with them a simple meal of preparation for the Passover. Nevertheless, the Jewish Passover has greatly influenced the Christian celebration of Holy Communion. The Passover meal was to remind the Hebrew of his days of liberation from Egyptian slavery.

The Feast of Weeks, like the other celebrations, was undoubtedly connected originally with agricultural rites of planting and harvesting. There is nothing in the O.T. to suggest the significance of this festival apart from its identification with the ingathering of the harvest. It was later connected by the Christian Church with the observance of Pentecost.

The Feast of Booths lasted for seven days after the harvest. During this time the community lived in booths, or huts, and the people were reminded of the days spent in wandering in the wilderness. But all of these celebrations were joyous occasions. It seems to be characteristic of Hebrew thinking that even in moments of great joy they remind themselves of more unpleasant scenes. There is a modern custom that during the marriage ceremony the bridegroom crushes a glass sphere, and the Rabbi says: "Even in our supreme happiness at this joyous occasion we remind ourselves of the suffering Jews throughout the world."

The final injunctions of this chapter concern the establishment of justice in every community and prohibition against erecting any symbol that might be suggestive of the symbols of Baalism (vv. 18-22).

141

Reading 87: Deuteronomy 17:2-20

We should call the provisions of this chapter and the ones that follow "Civil Law." The Hebrews made no distinction between the religious and secular as we do. Theirs was a religious community, and therefore all Law had religious significance.

The Law of Witnesses (vv. 6-7) has continued down to modern times. A man could not be convicted unless at least two witnesses agreed in their testimony against him. We still require at least two witnesses for many legal documents and transactions, such as marriages, the transfer of real estate, the attesting of a will, and the like. We are reminded also that it was this provision of the Deuteronomic Law that caused concern at the trial of Jesus (Mt. 26:59-61), for the priests had difficulty in getting the legal number of witnesses to testify against Jesus. According to Josephus, women and slaves were the only people who could not be used as witnesses.

The Law of Appeal is given in vv. 8-13. If the decision handed down by the local judge was not satisfactory, appeal could be made to Jerusalem, but that decision was final. If a man failed to heed that decision, he was to be put to death. This was a means of enforcing the authority of the court of appeals in Jerusalem.

Regulations concerning the king indicate that they must surely have been written in the light of the experience of the country during the days of Solomon. Six conditions are placed upon the king. He must not be a foreigner. He must not trade in horses. He must not have too many wives. He must not have too much gold or silver. He must know the religious Law. He must not consider himself exempt from the provisions of the Law simply because he is king.

Solomon was not a foreigner, but he violated most of the remainder of these standards. It was this that caused the people to turn against the monarchy. Solomon was a great trader in horses. The provision concerns trading, not the amassing of cavalry. Stables have been found at Megiddo

(Armageddon) which indicate the enormous number of horses traded by Solomon between Egypt and the northern countries. He also had the largest collection of wives of any man who served as king of the Hebrews. The number of wives a man had gave him prestige and was an index of his wealth. In addition, it was the custom to make treaties through marriage. When Solomon wanted a treaty with a foreign country, it was easily arranged through marriage (see 1 Kings 3:1). But this meant also that foreign custom made its way into the land of Palestine, for Solomon built special places of worship for his foreign wives (1 Kings 11:1-5).

Nowhere else in Hebrew Law is such control of the king provided for. It is in harmony with the general purpose of keeping the religion of Israel free from foreign influence.

Reading 88: Deuteronomy 18:1-22

The first paragraphs of this chapter provide for the support of the Levitical priests. They designate parts of the animals being sacrificed, and other products, which are to be given to the priesthood. In addition, it is provided that if a Levite leaves his old community and goes to Jerusalem he shall retain his prerogatives in his own town but he shall also share on an equal basis with the priests in Jerusalem. This is one part of the Deuteronomic Code that was not put into effect in the reform of Josiah (2 Kings 23:9). This may have been due to the self-interest of the priests already in residence at Jerusalem.

The distinction between sorcery and prophecy is made clear. The Hebrews are to have no traffic with any of the nine forms of superstition in vv. 10-11. The purport of this passage is that always there will be men who will be guided by God and who can give direction to the people. Since these words are placed on the lips of Moses, Moses is here recognized as a prophet, a title given him only in the later writings. The test of the prophet is simple: if what he says comes to pass then he is speaking the truth, otherwise he is a false messenger. Jeremiah denounces those individuals

143

who speak falsely, those prophets who deal in lying dreams (Jer. 23:30-40).

Hebrew prophecy had a long history, and during the years there were changing ideas of what actually constituted prophecy. The standard set forth in these verses is not on the highest level as far as function is concerned, for the main responsibility of the prophet according to this standard is to utter oracles or reveal visions that have come from God. The work of the greatest prophets in the eighth to sixth centuries had little to do with oracles and visions. Their messages came out of their knowledge of the people and of current evil practices, and as they prayed about these problems they were inspired of God to speak out. Their main concern was to examine the moral problems of their own day, to prick the consciences of leaders and people, and to raise the community to higher levels of moral and religious responsibility. Hebrew prophecy was growing in stature in the days of the composition of Deuteronomy, and the Law of Deuteronomy was stimulated by the prophets; but the picture of prophecy given in this book is not as great as prophecy had come to be. There is agreement, however, between the great prophets and this writing at this point, that the true prophet is a man of God and speaks only those things that are inspired of God.

Reading 89: Deuteronomy 19:1-21

Further details are given now for the control of the "cities of refuge." Here is an attempt to bridge the gap between two traditions, one of which designated three such cities, the other six (Deut. 4:41-43, Num. 35:9-34). Specific example is given of accidental killing (vv. 4-6), so that judges can be guided in their decisions. It is also provided that the known guilty person must not be permitted the safety of the city of refuge. Note, however, that his accusers have no right to enter the city to take him, but the elders of the city of refuge must deliver the guilty man into the custody of the avenger. This provision was wise, for it guarded against violence within the cities of refuge;

if violence had been permitted, these cities would have lost their significance.

V. 14 deals with landmarks. They had been placed in position by earlier people and were not to be moved. This was because such landmarks, usually great stones, were the only means of guarding property boundaries. The Egyptians had early devised a means of measurement of lands and a simple system of land survey. The Babylonians had continued to use the old method of putting a boulder, often inscribed with a curse upon the man who should move it, at the corners of the property. The Hammurabi Code had strict penalties for the removal of the landmark. Apparently it was a real problem, for Hosea likens the princes of Judah to those who remove boundaries. The crime of changing boundaries was so great that Hosea's condemnation of the princes was severe. The procedure followed was to remove the boundaries during the night, and when morning came little could be done, because the only test for determining property lines was the boundary stone itself. Only in Deuteronomy is this problem considered.

The problem of the false witness is considered in vv. 16-21. The man who tries to use Law falsely to pay a grudge is to be punished to the extent of the punishment that might have been meted out to the innocent victim. The effect of this law was to insure that testimony at law would be dependable, and that scoundrels would quickly be exterminated from the community.

Reading 90: Deuteronomy 20:1-20; 21:10-14

The Law of Warfare treats three separate problems. First is manpower. Because of the problem of morale, only those shall go into battle who are unafraid. Certain individuals in society are to be excused from warfare: the man who has built a new house but has not yet dedicated it, the man who has planted a vineyard but has not benefited from its fruit, and the man who is engaged but not yet married. All are freed from service in order to finish their peacetime obligations.

Nowhere else is the dedication of the ordinary home referred to, but a man's name was associated with his dwelling, and presumably this association followed formal dedication.

The Hebrew term used in connection with the vineyard is "to profane," for the new vineyard was considered "sacred" until after the first bearing, which belonged to God. Then the vineyard was made available to the family and community. It was the responsibility of the planter to make the vineyard available in this way. The community life also needed to encourage newlyweds.

The Assyrians were known for cruelty in warfare, and Israel suffered at their hands a number of times. The provisions given next are to guard against Israel's becoming as cruel as Assyria and to prevent atrocities of warfare. To us these provisions still seem cruel, but in the light of history the Hebrews had progressed far beyond their neighbors. Peace was to be offered to the besieged city immediately, and only after offers had been rejected were the armies to proceed with exterminating the city. Atrocities are not sanctioned or permitted. Men are to be killed, and the women taken captive for slaves. Compare the pictures given by Amos (1:3, 13) and Hosea (13:16). In the event that a soldier saw a beautiful captive woman and desired her for marriage there were certain formalities to be observed (vv. 10-13), and if the agreement failed she was to go free.

In besieging a city the Hebrews should take care to protect the fruit trees, and only nonfruit trees were to be used in the construction of battlements and fortifications.

All warfare was considered holy by the Hebrews. It is for this reason that the priest was to come to the armies before they started out in battle. His task was twofold. First, he must give courage to the soldiers; second, he must give them the conviction that God is going with them and will bring victory to them. This is the only instance in Hebrew Law where the priest is given this responsibility. It is at this point that there is often conflict in modern times between church and state. The church has insisted that men in war

146

as well as in peace need the aid that religion can give in order to become better men. The state has been concerned that the chaplain shall build the morale of men so that they can be better soldiers. The problem is still unsolved, even in church circles.

Reading 91: Deuteronomy 21:1-9, 15-23

Unsolved murder is a problem in any community. For the Hebrews it was doubly difficult, for they had the conviction that the community was under divine displeasure as long as murder went unavenged. An unworked heifer was to be sacrificed by having its neck broken near a running stream. The priests were then to "wash their hands in innocency." Compare the action of Pilate at the trial of Jesus (Mt. 27:24). Nowhere else in Hebrew Law is this provision made, and its purpose was probably to forestall blood revenge. A custom among the Arabs put the guilt for homicide upon the nearest homestead or the nearest village, but to prevent vengeance from the murdered man's tribe the people could swear under oath that they were innocent.

Another problem treated only by Deuteronomy is that of the rights of inheritance by the first-born son. Two portions of the property were to be designated to the first-born. This law does not mean that it established the custom, simply that it recognized a practice that had grown up among the Hebrews. Is this the reason that Elisha asked for a double-portion of the spirit of Elijah? Did he consider that he should be treated as a first-born son? A man could have more than one wife, but that frequently led to difficulty in the matter of inheritance (see Gen. 29:30-31). He also had power to bequeath his property as he desired, but there were certain restrictions recognized by custom. It is not indicated whether a will could be broken in case a man did not conform to pattern in designating the portions to be received by his heirs-at-law.

The son who refused obedience and was rebellious was to be formally charged with the crime by his parents at

147

the gate of the city. The gateway of the city usually contained an inner and an outer gate, and between them was the seat of the judges. It was here that the judges sat, and near by was the market place, the only open space in the city in which there could be a public gathering. The punishment seems severe, and it is an instance of the supreme authority of parents in the Hebrew system. Both father and mother have voice in the matter, but their charges are not open to question.

The closing verses of this chapter refer to special disgrace that could be heaped upon a criminal. This is not death by crucifixion or hanging, but it was the custom to kill a criminal, usually by stoning, and then after his death to impale his body upon a stake as a special public disgrace. The provision in these verses is that such impaling shall be confined to daylight hours. The body is not to remain on the stake overnight, but must be taken down and buried. This may have arisen from the fact that an exposed body would not be free from attack by animals if left overnight. Justice, but nothing beyond that, is a constant keynote in Deuteronomic legislation.

Reading 92: Deuteronomy 22:1-30

This is an expansion of the Covenant Code in Ex. 21–23, particularly of Ex. 23:4f. The word "brother" is inserted in v. 1 and is used in the sense of "fellow countryman." The provision (v. 5) against women's wearing men's things included more than ordinary garments. Anything that was considered a man's possession—weapons, tools, jewels, ornaments, and vessels—was included in this prohibition. Neither could men wear women's clothing. The provision was made to guard against the simulation of sexes well known in Canaanite and Syrian religious practices.

A new house was to have a parapet. This regulation appears for the first time in Deuteronomy. It was made because the houses of Palestine had flat roofs and in hot weather the roof made the most acceptable place to rest or sleep. A man falling from the roof could be seriously injured, and the man who had not guarded against such an accident by building a parapet was guilty. This regulation would have no significance to people living in the desert, and must have come into existence after men lived in cities, probably after someone had fallen from a roof.

Mixtures are not permitted (vv. 9-11), probably on the principle that man must not combine those things that the Creator has made separate.

Tassels for the corners of the cloak are mentioned in v. 12, but are treated more fully in Num. 15:37-41. The twisted threads, later of white wool, were fastened to the garment with a blue or purple cord.

Laws regulating marriage and chastity are stated in vv. 13-30. The first concerns the establishment of evidence of the bride's virginity. It is still the custom among Semitic tribes that the blood stained cloth from the nuptial bed shall be retained by the bride's parents in case of later dispute. The custom seems crude to us, but it must be remembered that there is a more realistic attitude toward mating in the Orient, and that a bride's dowry is based upon the virginity of the bride. This law is designed to protect the woman against false charges.

The penalty for adultery is death for both parties (v. 22). In the verses that follow, regulations are given concerning sex offenses of various sorts. The basis is that of preserving the sanctity of marriage, and every effort is made to see that justice is carried out.

Reading 93: Deuteronomy 24:1-22

Remarriage to a former wife is not permitted if she has in the meantime been married to someone else. So far as her first husband is concerned, he gave her a divorce because there was fault in her (v. 1); therefore her second marriage to him would be adultery (v. 4).

An upper millstone or a hand mill could not be given or taken as a pledge for a loan. To permit such a transaction would be to deprive a family of its daily bread. The

149

mill is used constantly in Palestine, and one of the first tasks of the day is to grind grain for the daily supply of food.

Kidnaping (v. 7) was punishable by death.

The borrowing of money was carefully regulated, and vv. 10-15 provide protection for the borrower. The creditor is to allow the borrower to decide what article he will give in pledge for the repayment of the loan. Interest is not mentioned, but if the loan was to a fellow countryman no interest was permitted. The poor people must have the special concession that clothing is to be returned at nightfall because they used their outer garments for bed covering. The payment of wages must be promptly made (vv. 14-15). Fathers are not to be killed with their children, and vice versa (cf. 2 Sam. 21:1-9; 2 Kings 14: 6; Jer. 31:30).

In vv. 19-22 specific provision is made for the poor. Grain missed in the harvesting is not to be recovered but is left for the poor. The same is true in gathering olives and grapes. The trees and vines are not to be picked over, and the poor are to be free to come into the fields and vineyards and help themselves.

There is evidence in all of these provisions that an attempt is being made to think in terms of human values. We cannot expect that in this early day there would be the same concern for human personality that we have in Christian circles today, but the standards in Deuteronomy are infinitely higher than the standards in the days of the patriarchs.

Written Work.—Write a paper on the subject "What Deuteronomy Teaches on How Men Should Live Together." Note the passages in which this matter comes up, making a list of the more important ones. Then set down the principles, or rules, which these passages indicate. At the close consider whether the N.T. goes beyond this, and list those N.T. passages that demand a higher standard than that of Deuteronomy.

Reading 94: Deuteronomy 25:1-19

Corporal punishment was to be carefully meted out. The strokes were to be counted, not given mercilessly or indiscriminately. In later times the custom prevailed to give not more than thirty-nine strokes, to insure against the possibility of a mistake (see 2 Cor. 11:24).

The principle that the laborer, even though an ox, is worthy of his hire is found only in Deuteronomy.

Levirate marriage (brother-in-law marriage) was a well-established practice in Israel, as well as among other peoples. See *Reading* 19 and *ABC,* p. 337. These verses give the clearest indication of the purpose of this custom—namely, to preserve the name of the brother throughout the generations by providing that there shall be offspring considered his and bearing his name. The refusal of a brother-in-law to meet his social and family obligation was ground for public contempt.

Honesty in business transactions depends upon a fixed system of weights and measures. The Hebrews never established official standards so far as we have been able to discover, but there were two systems in general use throughout much of their history. The Phoenicians had established one system and the Babylonians another. The traders had the trick of using the heavier system when they made purchases and the lighter system when they made sales, thus making an extra profit for themselves. This practice is definitely prohibited in vv. 13-16 (cf. Amos 8:5; Mic. 6:11; Ezek. 45:10).

Vengeance upon Amalek (vv. 17-19) is ruthless and indicates how low the standards really were between enemy countries.

Reading 95: Deuteronomy 26:1-19

Two rituals are given in this chapter which were to be performed periodically by the Hebrews. They form a suitable close to the chapters of legislation (12-25) and are probably of great age.

The purpose of the first is to remind the Hebrews constantly of their wonderful deliverance by God. It is an act of thanksgiving in which the people are reminded of their ancestor, destitute, foreign, and ready to perish until God had pity upon him. There is real disparagement here of their ancestral background, not to discredit their fore-fathers, but to magnify the greatness of their deliverance. The offering was to be the first fruits of the ground, and as the gift was given to the priest the words of the ritual were to be uttered by the giver. The object was that there would be thanksgiving not only for the harvest immediately brought in but for the complete history of the Hebrew people.

Similarly with the second ritual, which was to be performed every three years. The ritual was so worded that the bringer of the gift would in effect examine his whole past conduct and be able to say that he had always been obedient unto Jehovah. He then asked a blessing upon the future. Among other things he stated that he had carefully set aside the tithe, had not eaten while ceremonially unclean from mourning, had carefully observed all laws of taboo, had not made offerings to the dead, and had heeded the commands of God.

The final injunction of the chapter, to obey constantly the Law of God, ends with the promise that if they do obey they will be blessed and held in honor, for they will be known as a people consecrated to their God. There is once more the emphasis, so constant throughout the Deuteronomic Law, that the Covenant Law put responsibility upon God's people as well as upon God himself. Judaism has been distinguished for the centrality that religious Law has had in its thinking. Sometimes the emphasis has been upon the letter of the Law, and its spirit has been forgotten. There were great spirits, however, who caught the high challenge; and it is to these men that the world owes so much of its inspiration.

IX

A FINAL PICTURE OF MOSES
Deuteronomy 27:1–34:12

CH. 27 is an interruption of the second discourse of Moses, which is concluded in ch. 28. But this chapter and the remaining chapters of the book may appropriately be grouped together. They will give us an opportunity of looking again at the Great Lawgiver, Moses, whose personality has dominated the Books of the Law. Much of these closing chapters is in magnificent poetry and comes from dates earlier and later than the rest of the book of Deuteronomy. Glorious tribute is paid to Moses, and on his lips are placed words that agree with his character and his qualities of leadership; but we shall have difficulty in supposing that he could have had such complete knowledge of the history of the Hebrew people in the years after his death.

Much of this closing section is in the spirit of the priesthood, with its appeal to tradition, its emphasis upon ceremonial, and its stress upon the formally accepted Law Code. Yet we also have here the fire and fervor of the prophet confronting his people with the choice between the way of life and the way of death and challenging them to live in accordance with the highest standards they know.

There are some contradictions in the earlier provisions of the book of Deuteronomy; but, as we realize that this material comes from various times and perhaps different places, we can understand that there could easily be differences in details of religious practice and organization.

Reading 96: Deuteronomy 27:1-26

This chapter gives instructions relative to a symbolic acceptance by the nation of the Deuteronomic Code. It is an interruption of what has preceded and is presented in the third person. Four ceremonies are prescribed: (1) the inscription of Law on white-washed stones immediately upon entry into the promised land—vv. 2-4, 8; (2) the erection of an altar and the offering of sacrifices at the same place—vv. 5-7; (3) ratification of the new covenant—vv. 11-13; (4) the antiphonal reciting of twelve curses—vv. 14-26.

It is the first and second of these provisions that have caused the great controversy between the Jews and the Samaritans. Most of the Hebrew MSS. read that the Law and the altar shall be set up on Mount Ebal, while the Samaritan Pentateuch names Mount Gerizim. On this basis the Samaritans have claimed precedence for their Temple on Mount Gerizim over the rebuilt Temple of the Jews at Jerusalem. This conflicts with the rest of the book in its provision for worship only in Jerusalem.

The great stones to be erected were to be daubed with a whitewash or white plaster on which black pigment could be used for the inscriptions. The method was one used by Egyptians and later by the Greeks.

The setting and the curses of vv. 14-26 fit the description given in 11:26-32. The laws for whose violation curses are pronounced are found in the Covenant Code (Ex. 20:23–23:33), the Primitive Code (Ex. 34:17-26), and the Holiness Code (Lev. 17:1–26:46), with the exception of the law concerning boundary stones (v. 17).

These verses (14-26) have been recognized by Professor Pfeiffer as an old code formerly used by wanderers of the desert, and he would date this old code between 900 and 722 B.C. In any case, it is older than the actual formulation of the rest of the book of Deuteronomy.

Reading 97: Deuteronomy 28:1-46

This chapter is the close of the original Deuteronomic Code. It is a solemn declaration of the blessings and curses that will come to the nation as they observe or disregard the obligations of the Law. In its eloquence this chapter is one of the most striking in all Hebrew literature. Of its sixty-eight verses, only fourteen are devoted to the blessings; the rest are the curses that will come to the disobedient.

The original portion of this chapter is to be found in the poetical sections (vv. 3-6, 16-19). In these poetical fragments are briefly set forth the blessings and cursings so eloquently enlarged in the remainder of the chapter. Note the perfect contrasts between these two groups of verses.

Professor Leslie E. Fuller has summarized the teaching of this chapter and the whole philosophy of the book of Deuteronomy in these words: "Piety equals prosperity; sin equals suffering." That remained the orthodox position of Hebrew religion for many centuries, and is still held in much of Judaism today. It was in protest against this position that the book of Job was written. Yet it must be confessed that in general it is true if we think in terms of the social group and not of the individual. At the time of the formulation of the book of Deuteronomy the group was the important consideration, not the individual. The blessings promised to Israel were great material prosperity and supremacy over her political enemies. The curses include national and individual disaster, pain, and suffering.

It is a commentary upon the imagination that so much of the space is given over to descriptions of torment and punishment. Similarly, Dante's *Divine Comedy* devotes more space to the Inferno than to Paradise, and is more ingenious in its description of the former.

The blessings and curses are material, and the emphasis is upon the physical throughout. Is this not where so many people still want to place the emphasis? What are the great satisfactions in life? Can they be measured as we measure material wealth and possessions?

Reading 98: Deuteronomy 32:1-43

Except for the prose setting that precedes and follows this magnificent poem, there is no claim that Moses sang these lines. But we are not concerned as much with the

155

authorship as with content. The people are chided for their failures and there is sorrow that God's people have done so miserably, but there is a note of mercy and hope. The people of God will yet be triumphant because of the faithfulness of God.

Read carefully the translation that is given in *ABC*, pp. 341-42. The poem begins with a challenge to the entire universe to pay heed to the message. The contrast between God's unchanging righteousness and the people's corruption is then portrayed (vv. 4-6). God's care has been demonstrated (vv. 7-14), but "you do gorge yourself, and you do become fat and corpulent" (vv. 15-18—*American Trans.*). Punishment has been sent (vv. 19-22) and future punishment will be severe (vv. 23-25). Punishment has also been withheld out of regard for God's reputation among the enemies of the Hebrews (vv. 26-33), and the punishment due Israel will be turned against these enemies (vv. 34-42). Meantime God appeals to Israel and shows the folly of trusting strange gods (vv. 37-39). The concluding verse (43) is a shout of triumph and revenge over the enemies of God.

There are alternating notes of punishment and mercy. Note particularly v. 39, where God is designated both as the one who punishes and as the one who heals. These differing roles may arise from corresponding changes in man's attitude. At times he is deeply penitent, and again he shouts his defiance and self-sufficiency. In dealing with people we must keep in mind that life does not move forward on an even keel. There are times when men feel they are on the mountaintop, and there are others when they are in the valley of despair. It is the function of religion to minister to men under all circumstances, and whatever their experiences or moods may be.

The message of Jesus has made many changes in our understanding of the nature of God. We no longer picture God as being concerned about his own reputation, or having constantly changing moods. We lay stress upon the dependability and the love of God. God is always willing and ready for man to turn to him. Indeed, we can go much further in the light of the teachings of Jesus. God is yearning for the response of man's love to his divine love. Make notations in your notebook of the contrasts between our understanding of God through the teachings of the Christian church and the picture of God that is given in this poem.

We need to note, finally, that magnificent poetry does not necessarily give the highest teaching. Poetry can march into our very beings by the skill of its language, the beauty of its imagery, and the rhythm of its music; but its teaching may be on very low planes of thought. In many collections of religious poetry there is included the poem "Invictus" by William E. Henley. It has been set to music and is often sung in our churches. It appeals to our sense of independence and "rugged individualism," but as a matter of fact the poem is essentially pagan. We must guard constantly to see that ideas, no matter how enticingly dressed, shall not betray us into accepting less than the best.

Reading 99: Deuteronomy 33:1-29

This chapter is another conclusion to the words of Moses. It is a list of blessings, expressed in fine poetry, pronounced upon each tribe in turn. (Cf. Gen. 49.) This collection of blessings must have been made before the disappearance of the Northern Kingdom in 722-21 B.C. All tribes are included with the exception of Simeon. The half-tribes Ephraim and Manasseh are listed along with the blessing of Joseph. But Levi is still listed as a full tribe, though in the later lists of the tribes Levi is not so named.

This poem has rightly been called the "Blessing," for nowhere in the poem are curses mentioned. In turn the outstanding characteristics of the tribes are listed. The blessing of Reuben is one of the shortest; it simply expresses the hope that Reuben will not die out, though their number is small. For Judah there is a cry for help, and it implies that Judah has somehow been separated from the rest. Our knowledge of Hebrew history does not help us at this point.

157

The priestly functions of Levi are clearly indicated in (vv. 8-11). V. 12 is a short blessing upon Benjamin. The dwelling "between his shoulders" refers to the Temple on the hills of Jerusalem. This indicates that the poem was written sometime after the building of the Temple. The blessing pronounced upon Joseph and the tribes Ephraim and Manasseh is one of the longest (vv. 13-17). Fertility of the soil and great military strength are the blessings sought. Zebulun and Issachar are grouped together, and the description indicates the great wealth that has been amassed by these tribes from the sea. Gad (vv. 20-21) is praised and blessed for its leadership and for unwavering loyalty to Jehovah. The description of Dan can scarcely be called a blessing. It is simply a graphic description of the sudden forays for which Dan was known. The hope is expressed of Naphtali that the tribe will not always be confined to its mountain home but will benefit from the fertile plains to the south and an outlet to the sea. The final blessing concerns Asher. He is to be the favorite of the sons. The hope that his bars might be iron and bronze may come from the fact that Asher held the key to invasion from the north, the buffer state that protected the rest. If he could keep the bars locked, he would indeed be the favorite of the brothers.

The epilogue (vv. 26-29) is characteristic of the intense nationalism of the Hebrews expressed in so many periods of their history. God said, "Destroy," so Israel dwelt securely! And the closing words are: "Your foes shall come cringing to you, as you march over their heights" (*American Trans.*). We can understand this emphasis as we look at the long, hard struggle of the Hebrews to establish themselves. Armies were constantly marching through their territory. Constantly they were being used for a buffer state by the great nations of the Eastern world. There is more than compensation in these great poems. Far greater than narrow nationalism is the conviction that God had a destiny for the Hebrews, and that his purpose could be defeated neither by the strength of surrounding nations, for he would defeat them, nor by the failures of Israel, for he would win them back and despite their weaknesses would carry them forward to triumph.

Reading 100: Deuteronomy 34

The brief chapter at the close of Deuteronomy gives the close of the career of Moses. Read the closing chapter of Numbers, then this chapter, and see how completely they fit together. This chapter is dramatic. We are concerned now not with history but with the moving drama of a life. A man's work is done, and he surveys the accomplishment of the people who have been under his leadership. He sees also "the promised land," and the great days that lie ahead for this people, which they have approached under his guidance. There must have been satisfaction in a task well done and perhaps a regret that he could not go forward with them. This scene was graphically portrayed in the play *Green Pastures*. The final words (vv. 10-12) pay glowing tribute to this outstanding leader in the history of the Hebrew people.

What were his great contributions to the Hebrews, and through them to the world and to Christianity in particular? We can summarize his work under three heads. First, he started the Hebrew people on the way to their great understanding of God. It was with the challenge of the leadership of God that Moses led the tribes from Egyptian slavery. The concept of God in that early day was very crude, but the groundwork was laid upon which the prophets built an understanding of God that eventually was big enough to include all of mankind. The Hebrews have given to mankind the teaching that there is only one God and he is the Father of all mankind.

Moses gave to the Hebrew people the idea of a national destiny. We do not know just how many people he led through the wilderness, but we do know that it was around this nucleus that the Hebrew nation was later built and that the traditions of this small group became the traditions of a whole nation. It was left for David to build the national solidarity necessary for continuing national life. But

159

it was Moses who first implanted within the minds of the tribal groups the conviction that they had a destiny in history.

The third contribution of Moses was that of Law. We know that much of the Hebrew Law was of necessity written much later than the days of Moses, but the core of religious principle and human application was planted among the Hebrews by Moses. Much of the Hebrew Law has been accepted not only by Christians but by Western civilization and much of the rest of the world. Into the great law codes of modern civilization have gone the basic principles first enunciated by Moses and those who succeeded him. These are the reasons that Moses is revered by Jews and Christians alike. To have given to a people a sense of destiny and to the world an understanding of the nature of God and a basis for civil and religious Law—this is perhaps the most outstanding contribution that the world has ever seen.

Written Work.—Tell in your own words the contributions of Moses. In preparation for this paper, read *ABC*, pp. 253, 258-59, 303-4, 323, 327; Ex. 2:11-15, chs. 5-6; Num. 12, 14; Deut. 3, 9; and *Readings* 32, 35, 47, 67, 79.